4th + 5th Form

Basic Biology Questions for GCSE

National Curriculum Edition

Chris Rouan

Cheltenham College

Stanley Thornes (Publishers) Ltd

First published in 1986
Second edition published in 1989
National Curriculum edition published in 1994 by:
Stanley Thornes (Publishers) Ltd
Ellenborough House, Wellington Street, CHELTENHAM GL50 1YW

98 99 00 / 10 9 8 7 6 5 4

A catalogue record of this book is available from the British Library.

ISBN 0-7487-1726-9

Typeset by Blackpool Typesetting Services Limited.
Printed and bound in Great Britain by
TJ International Ltd, Padstow Cornwall

Contents

Preface v

Acknowledgements vi

Theme 1: The study of living things 1

1. The characteristics of living things 2
2. Naming and classifying living things 5
3. Collecting living things 8
4. Many forms of life 9
5. Bacteria, viruses and fungi 16
6. Some larger invertebrates 23
7. The vertebrates 25
8. Flowering plants 30

Theme 2: Living things and their environment 33

1. Cycles in nature 34
2. Feeding relationships 36
3. Where do organisms live? 40
4. The study of a habitat – an ecological survey 47
5. Changes through the year 48
6. Adaptation and survival 51
7. The soil 54
8. Decay 60
9. Populations 62
10. People and the environment 66

Theme 3: The basic organisation of living things 79

1. Plant and animal cells 80
2. Looking at cells 84
3. Tissues, organs and organisms 85
4. Movement in and out of cells 87
5. The chemistry of life 93
6. Enzymes 94

Theme 4: Life processes 97

1. Food and diet 98
2. Diet and good health 99
3. Teeth 102
4. Feeding in mammals 105

5. Feeding in invertebrates 106
6. Digesting food 108
7. Energy from food 113
8. Breathing and gaseous exchange 120
9. Living without oxygen 126
10. Blood 129
11. The heart and circulation 130
12. Photosynthesis 139
13. The structure of leaves 146
14. What do plants need to grow? 147
15. Transport in plants 149
16. The kidney and excretion 153
17. The skin and temperature control 158
18. The liver 161
19. The senses and responding to stimuli 163
20. The nervous system and reflex action 168
21. Chemical messengers 174
22. How plants respond to stimuli 179
23. The skeleton and movement 184

Theme 5: The continuity of life 189

1. Producing offspring 190
2. Reproduction in insects 191
3. Reproduction in vertebrates 195
4. Human reproductive systems 197
5. Human sexual development and the menstrual cycle 200
6. Pregnancy and birth 202
7. Preventing pregnancy 207
8. Sexual reproduction in flowering plants 210
9. Fruits and seeds 214
10. Reproduction without sex 218
11. Growth 223
12. Cell division 227
13. Heredity 234
14. More about genes 242
15. Variation 247
16. Selection and evolution 248

Theme 6: How organisms affect humans 257

1. Organisms as food for humans 258
2. Useful microbes 259
3. Food spoilage and its prevention 264
4. Microbes and disease 266
5. Parasites and humans 274
6. Insects, useful and harmful 277
7. Social insects 277

Preface to the National Curriculum Edition

Biological science, by the very nature of the subject, has an intrinsic appeal to children of all ages and abilities. However, interest can wane when faced with some of the more difficult demands of public examinations. Success and motivation go hand in hand.

The pressures on a teacher's time are considerabie and increasing. There is a constant demand for exercises that are effective, stimulating and also relatively easy to correct and evaluate.

This book has been written and more recently revised to help reinforce a basic biological knowledge and understanding required to meet the demands of the National Curriculum for Science at Sc2 Key Stage 4, and also the various extension topics essential to the award of a single subject GCSE in Biology.

It is important for pupils to feel confident as they progress through a subject and in designing a wide range of question styles and levels I hope to develop this confidence.

The aims of the book are as follows:

1. To provide a framework within which pupils can compile a useful set of correct notes by working through and completing the various assignments, either on their own or with the help of the teacher.
2. To develop a pupil-centred approach to learning.
3. To provide an opportunity to develop pupil skills in numeracy and literacy.
4. To provide stimulating and varied material which can reinforce and consolidate the basic biological facts needed for Key Stage 4, whether in tests or in homework or classwork assignments. It can also, of course, be used as a revision programme.
5. To provide material that can be useful to students studying biology independently.
6. To develop scientific skills such as observation, measurement, inter-pretation and application.
7. To provide graded material that can be used in a mixed-ability or streamed class, so that all pupils, it is to be hoped, will achieve some degree of success.
8. To provide material that is easy to use, easy to mark, and can be used in a wide variety of different ways by the teacher.

This new National Curriculum edition contains up-to-date material relating to all the major areas of biology. It also includes a selection of questions specific to the various extension topics, e.g. biotechnology, movement and support, the diversity of organisms, behaviour and survival, etc.

Anticipating the difficulty some pupils may have with diagrams, I have simplified many of those essential to syllabuses. Although there are questions asking pupils to copy diagrams I expect that in many cases they will be traced.

Chris Rouan
Cheltenham College, 1994

v

Acknowledgements

The author and publishers are grateful to Dr M. B. V. Roberts for permission to use the information on p. 18 and to base the following diagrams upon those used in *Biology for Life* (Thomas Nelson and Sons Ltd): pp. 22, 124, 137, 155, 158, 180–1 and 205.

We are also grateful to John Murray (Publishers) Ltd for permission to use an abridged passage from *A Pattern of Islands* by Arthur Grimble and to BBC Books for permission to use the passage from *Life on Earth* by David Attenborough on p. 249 and an adaptation of a passage from *The Ascent of Man* by J. Bronowski on p. 255.

Many people have helped in the production of this book and I would like to thank all those who have read the manuscript at its various stages for their constructive criticisms.

The idea of writing such a book was prompted by Michael Roberts and it is to him that I am particularly grateful, not only for his initial stimulus, but also for his constant support and encouragement. His comments on the manuscript were invaluable.

Finally it is with pleasure that I thank Stanley Thornes: for their enthusiasm, patience and good humour.

Theme 1

The Study of Living Things

1 The Characteristics of Living Things

Biology is the study of living things.

1 a) Make a list of the **characteristics of life** starting with 'Living things move'.

   b) Look at the drawings below and on the next page. For each organism write down the characteristics of life which you can *see* it possesses.

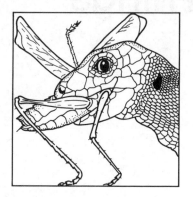 

 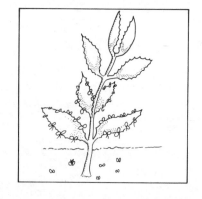

2 Match the words in the left-hand column with those in the right-hand column.

respiration	producing offspring
nutrition	movement from place to place
excretion	releasing energy from food
reproduction	responding to stimuli
sensitivity	feeding
locomotion	getting rid of poisonous waste

3 a)   Name *five* stimuli to which human beings are sensitive.

   b)   How do plants differ from animals in their response to stimuli?

4 From where do a) animals and b) plants obtain the substances that they need to increase in size?

5 Match the words in the left-hand column with those in the right-hand column to form sentences.

Autotrophs	feed on both plants and animals.
Heterotrophs	feed on other living things and do them harm, but do not always kill them.
Herbivores	feed on dead animal and plant material.
Carnivores	feed on plants.
Omnivores	are organisms like green plants which make their own food.
Parasites	are organisms like animals which need to eat ready-made organic food.
Saprotrophs (saprophytes)	feed on animals.

6 The table below lists **differences between animals and plants**. Copy and complete it by giving a reason for each difference.

Typical animal (e.g. a frog or a trout)	Typical plant (e.g. a buttercup or a French bean)	What is the reason for this difference?
Has feeding structures such as mouth and gut	Lacks feeding structures	
Lacks chlorophyll	Has chlorophyll	
Is not rooted in the ground	Is rooted in the ground	
Moves around	Does not move around	
Has nerves and muscles	Lacks nerves and muscles	
Has complex sense receptors such as eyes and ears	Lacks complex sense receptors	

7

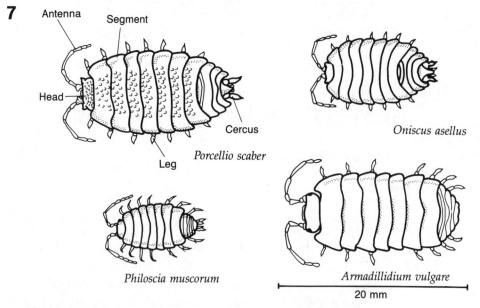

Porcellio scaber

Oniscus asellus

Philoscia muscorum

Armadillidium vulgare

20 mm

This is an exercise in observation.

a) Study the diagrams of the woodlice carefully, and then suggest *at least one* way in which each woodlouse differs from the other three. Ignore any differences in size.

Record your observations in a table with these headings.

Species	Observations

b) Why is size not a useful feature to choose when making such comparisons?

2 Naming and Classifying Living Things

1   Choose a), b), c) or d) to complete this sentence:

      To biologists, classification means . . .

a)   giving organisms a name.

b)   putting organisms into groups.

c)   identifying organisms.

d)   describing organisms.

2   Explain why biologists

a)   classify organisms

b)   give organisms a scientific name

3   Here is a list of the groups which biologists use to classify organisms:

    class   family   genus   kingdom   order   phylum   species

Rewrite the list in order of size, starting with the largest group.

4   Try to find out the scientific names of *five* different organisms.

5   a)   Look at the six illustrations of insects, labelled A–F. Use the key to identify each of the insects.

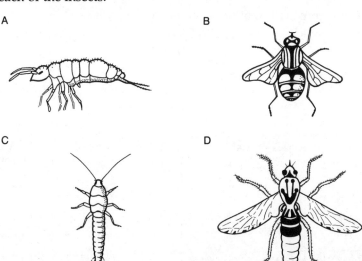

A

B

C

D

(continued overleaf)

E   F

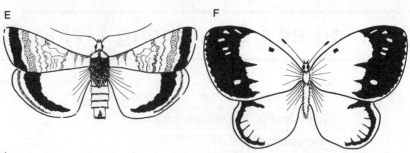

KEY

1. a)   wings absent   – go to number 2
   b)   wings present   – go to number 3

2. a)   three tail filaments   – silverfish
   b)   two tail filaments   – springtail

3. a)   one pair of wings   – go to number 4
   b)   two pairs of wings   – go to number 5

4. a)   end of abdomen pointed   – robber fly
   b)   end of abdomen not pointed – go to number 6

5. a)   club-shaped antennae   – clouded yellow butterfly
   b)   pointed antennae   – large yellow moth

6. a)   wings larger than body   – green lacewing
   b)   wings shorter than body   – hoverfly

b)   Look again at the illustrations of the six insects.

   i)   If you found one of these insects, what visible characteristics would help
        you to decide that it was an insect?

   ii) What visible characteristics helped you to identify insects A, B and C
        using the key?

6   Here is some information about the **arthropods**:

Phylum Arthropoda
Body divided into segments
Hard **exoskeleton**
Jointed limbs attached to body segments.

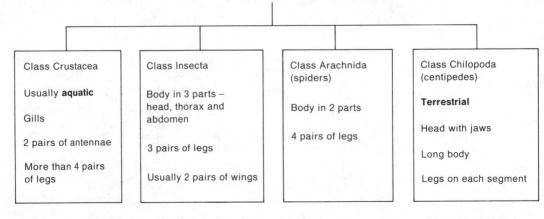

Class Crustacea	Class Insecta	Class Arachnida (spiders)	Class Chilopoda (centipedes)
Usually **aquatic**	Body in 3 parts – head, thorax and abdomen	Body in 2 parts	**Terrestrial**
Gills			Head with jaws
2 pairs of antennae	3 pairs of legs	4 pairs of legs	Long body
More than 4 pairs of legs	Usually 2 pairs of wings		Legs on each segment

a) Explain the meaning of the words:

i) exoskeleton   ii) aquatic   iii) terrestrial

b) Below are some drawings of arthropods. Use the information given to decide which class each of them belongs to. Record your answers in a table.

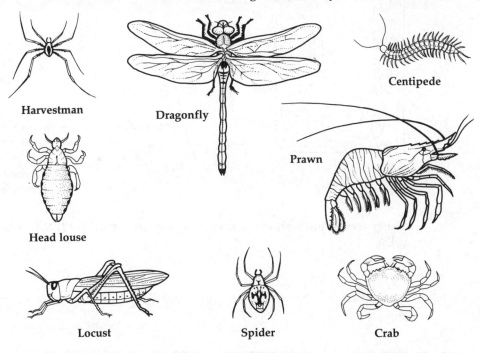

Harvestman

Dragonfly

Centipede

Head louse

Prawn

Locust

Spider

Crab

7 The diagrams below show six different plant and animal cells. (They are not drawn to the same scale.)

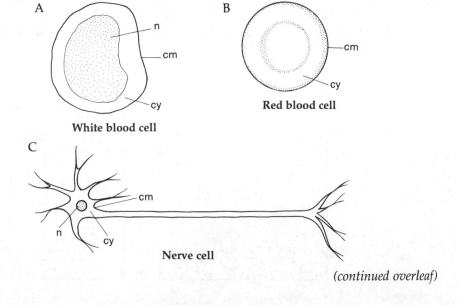

A

n

cm

cy

White blood cell

B

cm

cy

Red blood cell

C

cm

n

cy

Nerve cell

(continued overleaf)

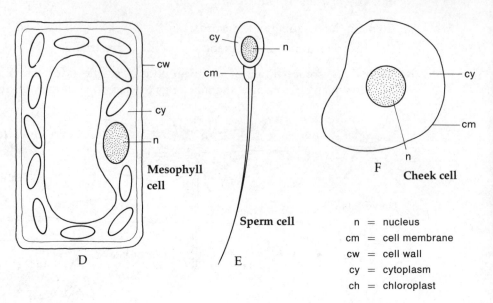

Mesophyll
cell

D

Sperm cell

E

F Cheek cell

n = nucleus
cm = cell membrane
cw = cell wall
cy = cytoplasm
ch = chloroplast

Using the features shown construct a key to correctly identify each of these cells.

3 Collecting Living Things

1 The diagrams below and at the top of the next page show pieces of apparatus you might use to collect living things.

Sweep net

Pooter

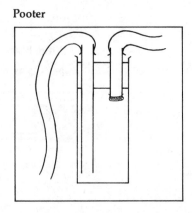

Pitfall trap

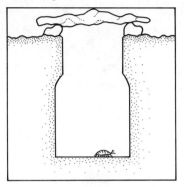

Plankton net

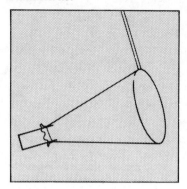

Beating-tray (or collecting-sheet)

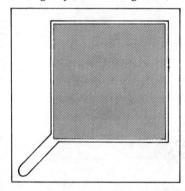

Mammal trap

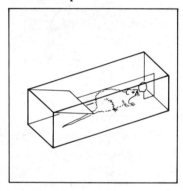

a) Briefly describe where and how you would use each one.

b) Describe *two* other methods of collecting organisms, one for water animals and one for land animals.

c) Make a list of at least *ten* other simple pieces of equipment that you might take with you when collecting living things.

4 Many Forms of Life

1 All living organisms are placed into one of six **kingdoms**. These are:

Viruses   Bacteria   Fungi   Protoctists   Plants   Animals

Into which kingdom would you place each of the following organisms? (They are not drawn to the same scale.)

a)

Bacteria

(continued overleaf)

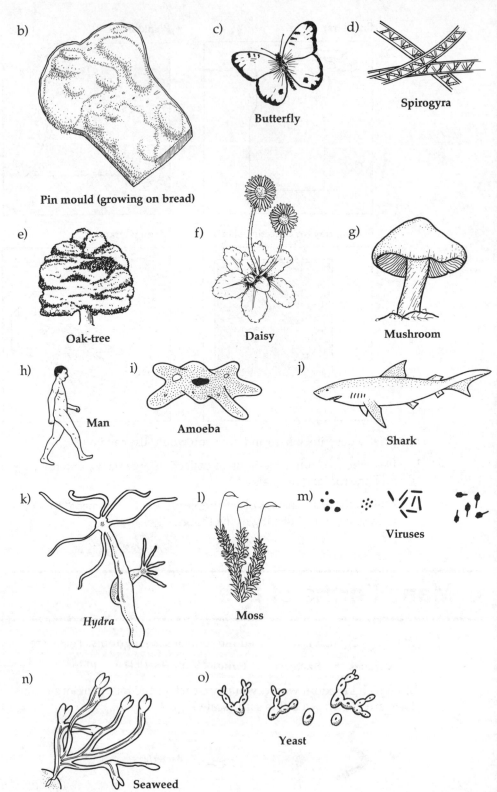

b)

Pin mould (growing on bread)

c)

Butterfly

d)

Spirogyra

e)

Oak-tree

f)

Daisy

g)

Mushroom

h)

Man

i)

Amoeba

j)

Shark

k)

Hydra

l)

Moss

m)

Viruses

n)

Seaweed

o)

Yeast

2   Each of the organisms shown below belong to the **Animal Kingdom**. They are not drawn to the same scale. Into which major group or **phylum** would you place each one? Choose your answers from the following list:

annelid worms   arthropods   cnidarians   echinoderms
flatworms   molluscs   vertebrates

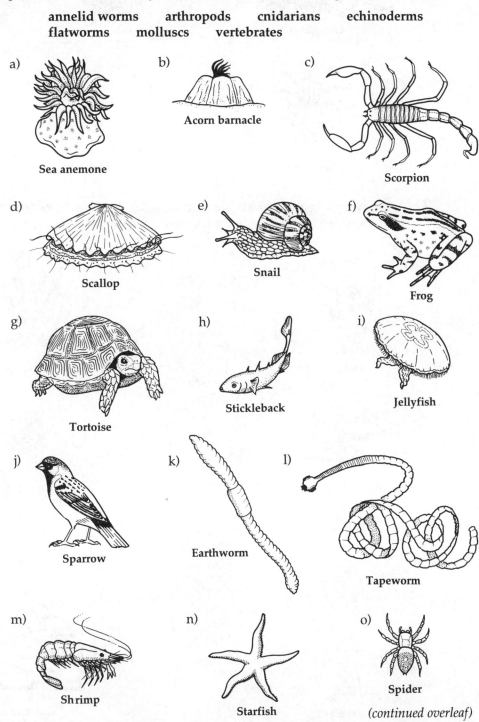

a)

Sea anemone

b)

Acorn barnacle

c)

Scorpion

d)

Scallop

e)

Snail

f)

Frog

g)

Tortoise

h)

Stickleback

i)

Jellyfish

j)

Sparrow

k)

Earthworm

l)

Tapeworm

m)

Shrimp

n)

Starfish

o)

Spider

(continued overleaf)

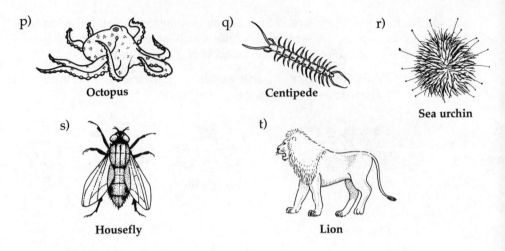

p) Octopus

q) Centipede

r) Sea urchin

s) Housefly

t) Lion

3 The drawings below (which are not to scale) illustrate a **variety of plants**. Study them and answer the questions which follow.

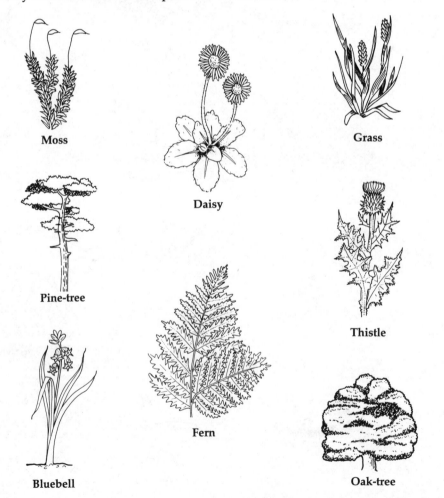

Moss

Daisy

Grass

Pine-tree

Fern

Thistle

Bluebell

Oak-tree

   a)   Which of the plants produce spores?

   b)   Which one has no true roots?

   c)   Which ones depend on water for reproduction?

   d)   Which spore producing plant has leaves with a cuticle and specialised transport tissue (xylem and phloem)?

   e)   Which of the plants is a conifer?

   f)   Which ones are flowering plants?

   g)   Which of the plants produce seeds?

   h)   Which of the flowering plants are
      i)   monocotyledons
      ii)   dicotyledons?

4 Each of the following statements describes characteristics of a particular group of living things. After reading the example, identify the groups described.

> *Example:* **The organism has a constant body temperature, forelimbs adapted for wings, a backbone, lays shelled eggs.**
>
> **It is a BIRD.**

   a)   Has no backbone, three parts to its body, six jointed legs.

   b)   Has a backbone, gills, no legs, lays many eggs.

   c)   Has hair, a constant body temperature, suckles its young.

   d)   Has no backbone, its body is long and divided into segments, no legs.

   e)   Has no backbone, two parts to its body, eight jointed legs.

   f)   Is evergreen, with cones for reproduction.

   g)   Has flowers for reproduction, broad leaves with branched veins, one main root.

   h)   Has a body made up of only one cell.

   i)   Has a mycelium of hyphae, no chlorophyll, spores.

   j)   Has simple leaves, no proper roots, no xylem or phloem, spores formed in capsules.

   k)   Has proper roots, stems and leaf-like fronds, spores.

5 a) Which of the plants shown in the diagram below is a monocotyledonous plant and which is a dicotyledonous plant?

    b) What features of the plants shown in the diagram support your answer?

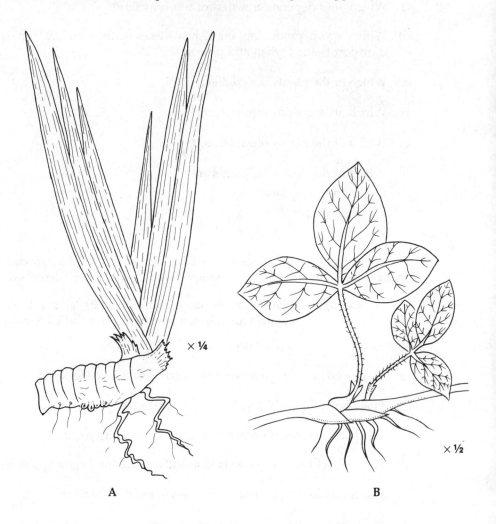

A   B

× ¼   × ½

6 The illustrations below represent various **vertebrates**. (They are not drawn to the same scale.)

Shark   Frog

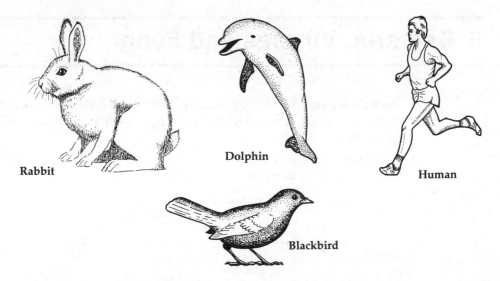

Rabbit

Dolphin

Human

Blackbird

Answer these questions about the animals shown:

a) Which of the animals lay eggs?

b) Which of the animals are mammals?

c) i)   Which of the animals has very light hollow bones?

   ii) Give a reason why hollow bones are important to this animal.

d) Which animal breathes through gills?

e) All the animals shown are vertebrates. What does the word 'vertebrate' mean?

f) Which *two* of the animals cannot control their body temperature?

7   In each of the lists below choose one organism that is the **odd one out**. Give a biological reason for your choice.

a) sparrow, sea anemone, lichen, shrimp, octopus

b) earthworm, slug, shrimp, centipede, eel

c) ladybird, snail, wood-louse, millipede, spider

d) horse, dolphin, camel, whale, penguin

e) oak, sycamore, beech, pine, ash

f) rat, lion, kangaroo, elephant, rabbit

g) bluebell, fern, bracken, moss, seaweed

h) newt, lizard, frog, toad, salamander

i) cod, salmon, trout, shark, dolphin

j) foxglove, grass, primrose, dandelion, buttercup

5 Bacteria, Viruses and Fungi

1 a) Bacteria are very small cells, and may have many different shapes. A single bacterium cannot be seen with the naked eye; so what makes it possible for us to see them?

b) Construct a table with the headings shown below to show as many *different types of bacteria* as you can.

Headings:	Shape	Name	Example of a disease caused by them
Example:	O	coccus	sore throat

2 a) Bacteria are microscopic organisms. They cannot be seen with the naked eye. Small units are needed to measure their length. The best units to use are **micrometres**. A micrometre is one thousandth of a millimetre.

$$\textbf{1000 micrometres} = \textbf{1 millimetre}$$

$$\textbf{1000}\ \mu\textbf{m} = \textbf{1 mm}$$

i) How many micrometres are there in one metre?

ii) The diagrams below show two types of bacteria magnified 4000 times. What is the actual length in micrometres of the two types of bacteria?

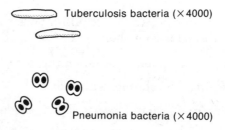

Tuberculosis bacteria (×4000)

Pneumonia bacteria (×4000)

b) Smaller things such as viruses are measured in units called nanometres. A nanometre is one millionth of a millimetre.

$$\textbf{1 000 000 nanometres} = \textbf{1 millimetre}$$

$$\textbf{1 000 000 nm} = \textbf{1 mm}$$

i) How many nanometres are there in one micrometre?

ii) How many nanometres are there in one metre?

iii) By how many times has the mumps virus been enlarged in the diagram below?

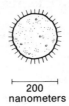

├─────┤
200
nanometers

c) Place these units in order, starting with the smallest unit and ending with the largest:

kilometre   metre   micrometre   millimetre   nanometre

3 The diagrams show three microorganisms. One shows yeast, one shows a bacterium and the third shows a virus.

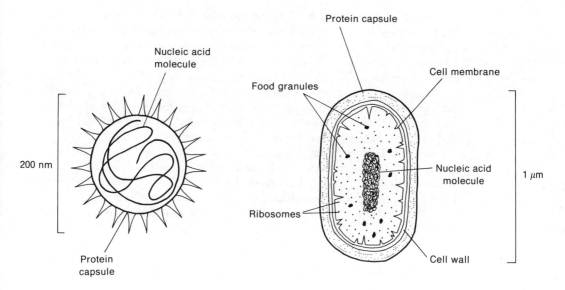

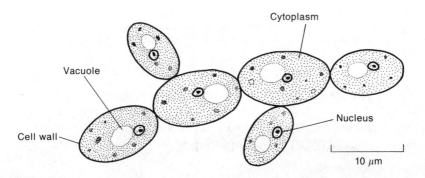

a) Copy the diagrams and correctly identify each one.

b) Give *two* features which the virus and the bacterium have in common.

c) Give *two* features which the bacterium and yeast have in common.

d) Give *four* ways in which the virus differs from the yeast cell.

e) Give *four* ways in which the bacterium differs from a plant cell.

f) Some microorganisms can be used to produce food for humans. Name *two* microorganisms which are used in this way and for each one name one food which it produces.

4 Carefully read this passage about **how we can grow bacteria**, and then answer the questions.

> To grow bacteria they must be given moisture, warmth and plenty of food. Many years ago it was discovered that they will grow on the surface of a jelly-like material obtained from sea weed. This is called **agar**. Various food substances are added to the agar: this makes it an ideal **nutrient medium** in which to grow, or **culture**, bacteria.
>
> The agar is usually put in a shallow **petri dish**. This must be sterilised beforehand and kept covered, otherwise moulds may grow on the agar. To speed up their growth the bacteria should be kept warm: this is best achieved by putting the petri dish in an **incubator**, a warm box in which the temperature can be kept constant.
>
> Now suppose you put some bacteria on the surface of some nutrient agar. In the course of the next day or two the bacteria multiply into **colonies**. Each colony consists of thousands of bacteria clumped together. The individual bacteria are too small to be seen with the naked eye, but the colonies are clearly visible.
>
> Bacterial colonies vary in size, shape and colour, according to the type of bacteria which give rise to them.

a) What conditions do bacteria need in order to grow?

b) What is agar?

c) What is added to agar to make it an 'ideal nutrient medium'?

d) Explain the meanings of the following words as used in the passage:

      culture   **sterile**   **colony**   **incubator**

e) Why is it important to wash your hands thoroughly
    i)   before starting to culture bacteria?
    ii)   after handling the plates?

f) In order to culture microbes safely, the following procedure is used. Copy the table below and for each stage give an appropriate reason.

Procedure	Reason
Petri dishes and growth media are sterilised	
An inoculating loop is used to transfer microbes	
The loop is passed through a Bunsen flame before and after use	
The lid of the petri dish is sealed with adhesive tape after inoculation	
In schools cultures are incubated at a maximum of 25 °C	
After use the cultures are heated in an autoclave (pressure cooker) or put into very strong disinfectant	

5 **Either:** Describe an experiment that you would carry out to find out what sort of bacteria occur in different places.

Or: Describe how you would carry out an experiment to find out if there are bacteria in soil.

You should include in your answer details of any controls that are necessary, and the precautions, if any, that must be taken.

6 Copy and complete the sentences below about **the way bacteria obtain their food**. Use words from the following list:

> parasites   photosynthesis   decay   saprotrophs   disease
> chemosynthesis   chlorophyll

a) Bacteria called _____ obtain food from dead organisms and help bring about _____ .

b) Bacteria called _____ feed on living organisms and cause _____ .

c) Bacteria which make their own food using light energy from the sun and _____ carry out a type of _____ .

d) Some bacteria make their own food using energy from chemical reactions. This process is called _____ .

7 Decide whether each of these statements about **bacteria and viruses** is true or false. Copy the true statements and rewrite the false ones correctly.

a) A typical bacterium is about a thousandth of a metre wide.

b) A nanometre is one millionth of a millimetre.

c) A typical virus is about 100 nm wide.

d) Bacteria are smaller than viruses.

e) Viruses can only be seen with an electron microscope.

f) Bacteria cannot be seen with a light microscope.

g) Viruses are simpler than any other organisms, including bacteria.

h) Bacteria always cause disease.

i) Viruses always cause disease.

j) Viruses are the smallest living things yet discovered.

k) The common cold is caused by a bacterium.

l) Mumps, smallpox, measles, polio and influenza are all caused by viruses.

m) Viruses can only live inside other living cells.

n) All viruses are the same shape.

o) Viruses form crystals.

8 Many bacteria are able to form spores. How does this help them to survive?

9 This question is about **the virus life cycle**.

a) Rearrange into the correct order and then copy the diagrams below to show how a virus reproduces.

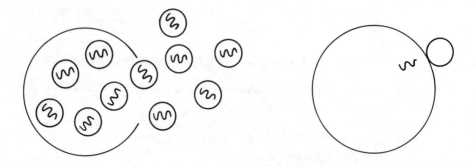

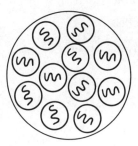 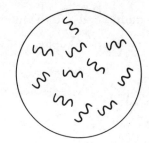 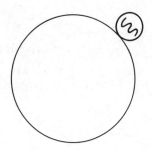

b) Describe what is happening at each stage using the statements given below.

The viral nucleic acid
penetrates the cell
and takes control

The virus turns the
host cell into a
virus producing
factory

The virus becomes attached
to the surface of a
living cell

Hundreds of new virus
particles are then
released from the body
cell, each one ready to
infect new cells

New viruses are
assembled using
materials from
the host cell

c) Use the above information to explain why all viruses are harmful.

10 Match the groups of words in the left-hand and right-hand columns to form
sentences that describe **pin mould fungus**.

a) **Some fungi are parasites but**   enzymes which digest the food.

b) **Saprotrophs feed on**   dead material and bring about
                                                        decay.

c) **Pin mould is commonly found
    growing**   a spore case at the tip.

d) **Fungi produce large numbers of**   the pin mould is a saprotroph.

e) **When a spore lands on a suitable
    surface**   the spores are released.

f) **The threads, or hyphae,**   small light spores which float in
                                                        the air.

g) **The mass of threads is called**   it bursts open and a thread grows
                                                        out.

h) **The threads produce**   by diffusion.

i) **The digested food is**   on stale bread.

j) **Pin mould threads obtain oxygen
    and get rid of carbon dioxide**   a mycelium.

k) **Some threads grow upwards and
    each produces**   absorbed by the threads.

l) **When the spore case bursts open**   grow over the surface of their food.

11 Copy this diagram of **pin mould** and add the following labels:

       horizontal hyphae   **vertical hyphae**   **spore case**   **spores**

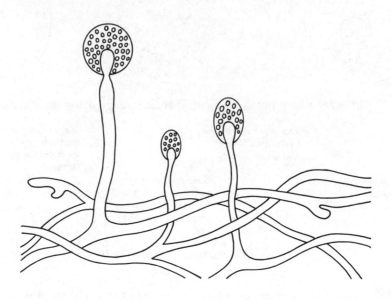

12 Look at the diagram below, which shows **part of a thread of pin mould**.

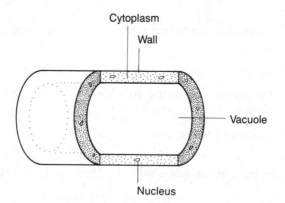

a) Which of the following features of the thread are found in plants?

    i)   vacuole

    ii)   wall

    iii) absence of chlorophyll

    iv) no division into cells

b) Which of the features in a) above make pin mould different from plants?

13 Explain why

    a)   pin mould is not green

    b)   pin mould needs to produce large numbers of spores

    c)   the spores are very light

    d)   pin mould will not grow on dry food

    e)   the threads of pin mould always stay near the surface of the food

6 Some Larger Invertebrates

1 Copy and complete these sentences:

    a)   Invertebrates are animals which do not have _____ .

    b)   The earthworm belongs to the major group (phylum) of invertebrates called the _____ .

    c)   Insects belong to the major group of invertebrates called the _____ .

2 Consider the diagram of the **earthworm**. How do the following features of earthworms help them to burrow through the soil?

    a)   The body has a streamlined shape.

    b)   The skin is soft and slimy.

    c)   There are pairs of bristles on each segment.

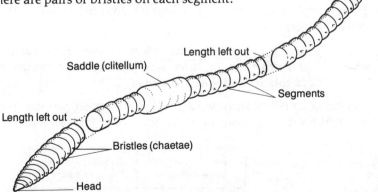

3 Copy the paragraph below about the **structure of the earthworm**. Choose words from the following list and fill in the gaps:

>   mouth   dorsal   segments   anus   skin   blood   bristles
>   saddle   head   chaetae   reproduction

The body of the earthworm is divided into rings or _____ . The front end is the _____ and it has an opening called the _____ . The back end has an opening called the _____ . About a third of the way along the body is a region called the _____ which plays an important part in _____ . Sticking out of each segment are four pairs of stiff _____ called _____ . Along the top or _____ side of the body, just below the _____ , runs a dark red _____ vessel.

4 Match the words in the left-hand column with those in the right-hand column.

>   anterior   bottom
>   posterior   front
>   dorsal   back
>   ventral   top

5 What does the earthworm use the following structures for?

a) mouth

b) gizzard

c) anus

d) circular and longitudinal muscles

e) bristles

f) saddle

g) excretory organs

h) skin

6 The following are features of **insects**. Some of them are possessed by all arthropods (the phylum or major group to which insects belong) and others are possessed by insects only.

>   jointed legs   three pairs of legs   usually two pairs of wings
>   segmented body   three parts to body (head, thorax and abdomen)
>   hard cuticle   jointed antennae

Construct a table to show which of the features are possessed by all arthropods, and which features belong only to insects. Your table should look like this:

Features possessed by all arthopods	Features possessed only by insects

7 Draw a large diagram of an **adult insect** you have studied. Include the name of the insect, its sex, and the scale of your diagram. Add the following labels to your diagram:

walking legs   eye   antenna   wings   mouthparts   head
thorax   abdomen

8 Answer these questions about **the insect cuticle**:

a) What is the cuticle made of?

b) What are the functions of the cuticle?

c) Why is the cuticle called an exoskeleton?

d) What is the disadvantage of having a cuticle?

> *Did You Know?*
> There are more species of insect in the world than of all the other animals put together.

7 The Vertebrates

1 Complete these sentences:

a) The vertebrates are animals with _____ .

b) The five classes of vertebrates are _____ , _____ , _____ , _____ and _____ .

2 For each of the five vertebrate classes answer the questions a) to e) below.

a) Are they warm- or cold-blooded?

b) State whether the body is covered with hair, scales, feathers or slime.

c) Do the adults breathe by means of gills or lungs?

d) Do the adults move by means of fins, legs or wings?

e) Do they lay eggs? If so, do the eggs have shells?

3 Copy this outline of a **bony fish**.

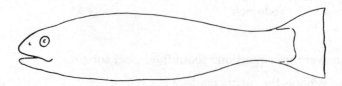

a) On the outline draw in and label

    i)   the gill cover

    ii)   the lateral line

    iii)   a dorsal fin

    iv)   a pectoral fin

    v)   a pelvic fin

    vi)   a ventral fin

b) Label also the tail, nostril, eye and mouth.

4 Give the names of

a) two freshwater bony fishes

b) two sea-water bony fishes

c) two cartilaginous fishes

5 Explain how the following features of bony fishes make them well suited for life in water:

a) They are streamlined.

b) They possess gills.

c) They have fins.

d) They have a swim bladder.

6 Complete the following sentences by using either 'amphibians' or 'reptiles':

a) Frogs, toads and newts are _____ .

b) Snakes, lizards, crocodiles and tortoises are _____ .

c) The skin of _____ is smooth and slimy.

d) The skin of _____ is covered with scales.

e) _____ are well suited to life on dry land.

f) _____ must always live in damp places.

g) _____ use only lungs to breathe.

h) _____ use their skin and lungs for breathing.

i) The eggs of _____ are covered in jelly.

j) The eggs of _____ are covered in a leathery shell.

k) _____ mate in water.

l) The eggs of _____ are fertilised externally.

m) The eggs of _____ are fertilised internally.

n) _____ can regulate their body temperature to a large extent by their behaviour.

7 Below are some observations about **birds**; suggest why each feature helps birds to survive.

a) Birds have feathered wings.

b) Their bodies are streamlined.

c) Each toe ends in a claw.

d) Their eyes have a third eyelid.

e) The gizzard of seed-eating birds contains small stones.

f) Their bodies contain air sacs leading from the lungs.

g) Their bones are hollow.

h) They often preen their feathers.

i) They build nests.

j) They look after their young.

8 Study the illustrations of birds' beaks at the top of the next page, and complete the table below.

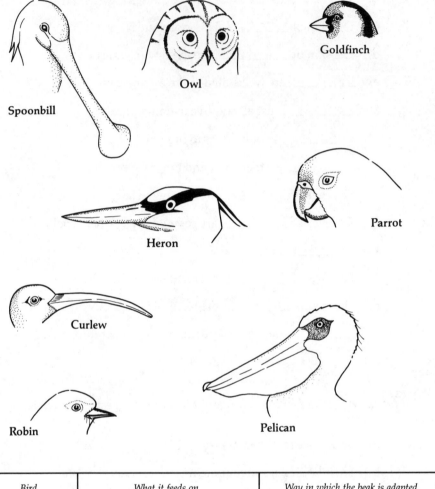

Bird	What it feeds on	Way in which the beak is adapted

9 a) Draw a large diagram of a flight feather and add the following labels:

      quill   vane   barbs

  b) List *four* functions of feathers.

  c) List the different ways in which a bird is adapted for flight.

10 Study the illustrations of birds' feet below and match each with one of the following descriptions of the bird:

a) catches prey

b) paddles along on water

c) wades through water

d) clings vertically to trees

e) hops along the ground

Can you think of birds that fit these descriptions?

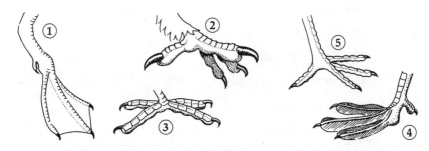

11 The diagram shows a cross-section through a wing and the air flow it creates as it cuts through the air.

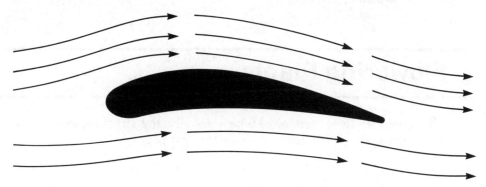

a) Copy the above diagram.

b) Describe how the sectional shape of the wing and the air flow it creates help to produce lift.

12 Match the words in the left-hand column with those in the right-hand column to produce sentences that describe some of the special features of **mammals**.

The teeth	separates the thorax and abdomen.
The pinna	are specialised for different jobs.
The diaphragm	produce milk for young.
The mammary glands	directs sound into the ear.
The middle ear	contains three small bones.

13 Answer the following questions:

    a)   Where are marsupial mammals mainly found?

    b)   What is the function (job) of the pouch in marsupial mammals?

    c)   What is the function of the placenta?

    d)   Are humans placental or marsupial mammals?

14 Give an example of each of the following:

    a)   a marsupial mammal

    b)   a bipedal mammal

    c)   a mammal with wings

    d)   a hairless mammal

    e)   a mammal that lays eggs

    f)   a mammal living entirely in water

    g)   a carnivorous mammal

    h)   a herbivorous mammal

    i)   a rodent mammal

    j)   a mammal with hoofs.

8 Flowering Plants

1 Complete these sentences, which describe **the structure of a flowering plant** such as the one in the diagram on the next page.

    a)   The plant is made up of two main parts, the _____ and the _____ .

    b)   The _____ is above the ground and the _____ is below the ground.

    c)   The main root is called the _____ .

    d)   Near the tip of each side root is a covering of _____ _____ .

    e)   At the tip of the shoot there is an _____ bud where growth takes place.

    f)   _____ are flat and green.

    g)   Each leaf is attached to the stem by a short _____ _____ .

    h)   Nodes are the points where _____ are attached to the stem.

    i)   The distance between two nodes is called an _____ .

    j)   The small bud at a node is called an _____ bud.

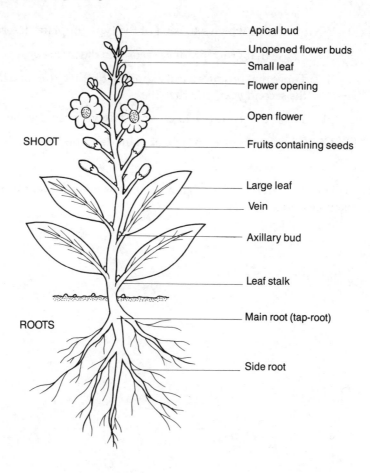

Apical bud
Unopened flower buds
Small leaf
Flower opening

Open flower

Fruits containing seeds

SHOOT

Large leaf

Vein

Axillary bud

Leaf stalk

Main root (tap-root)

ROOTS

Side root

2 Match the plants in the left-hand column with one of the descriptions in the right-hand column.

Plant	Description
Herbaceous plants	They contain quite a lot of wood and often have a bushy appearance.
Shrubs	They have a very woody stem called a trunk.
Trees	They are usually small with very little wood.

3 What jobs are carried out by

a) the stem?

b) the roots?

c) the leaves?

d) the flowers?

e) the fruits?

4 a) What name do we give to each of the types of plant described below?

    i)   Those that grow, produce seeds and die in one year

    ii)   Those that produce a leafy shoot in the first year, and flowers and seeds in the second year, and then die

    iii) Those that continue to grow and flower year after year

  b) Give an example of each type of plant described above.

5 Explain the difference between a **deciduous** and an **evergreen** tree and give *two* examples of each.

Theme 2

Living Things and Their Environment

1 Cycles in Nature

1 a) Copy the diagram below which summarises the **water cycle**. Fill in the boxes using the words provided.

evaporation   rainfall   sweating   transpiration   drainage

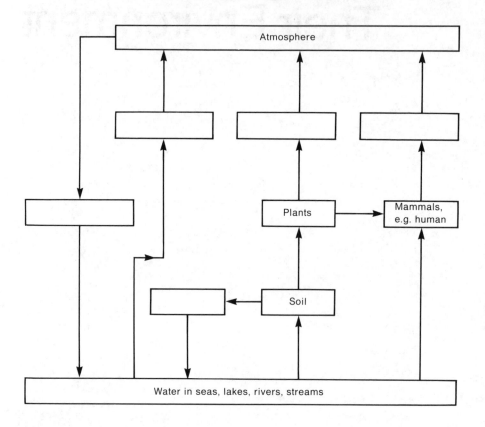

     b)   In what ways do animals and plants obtain water?

     c)   Why is water essential to life?

     d)   What is transpiration?

     e)   Why is the water cycle important to farmers?

     f)   What is the difference between fresh water and sea-water?

     g)   Name

         i)   *three* organisms that live in fresh water.

         ii)   *three* organisms that live in the sea.

2 a) Copy these sentences about the **carbon cycle**. Choose words from the following list and fill in the gaps. (The words may be used more than once.)

> plants   decay   respiration   animals   photosynthesis   combustion
> carbon dioxide

    i)   _____ use carbon dioxide and water to make sugars by the process of _____ .

    ii)   _____ and _____ break down sugars into carbon dioxide and water by the process of _____ .

    iii) When animals and plants die, their bodies _____ .

    iv) During the process of decay, microbes return _____ to the atmosphere.

    v)   Carbon dioxide is removed from the air by the process of _____ and put back into it by the processes of _____ and _____ .

    vi) When fossil fuels are burnt, carbon dioxide is returned to the atmosphere. This process is called _____ .

b) Name *two* fossil fuels. How are they formed?

c) Draw a diagram to show how the processes of **photosynthesis, respiration, combustion** and **decay** are involved in the carbon cycle.

3 Answer these questions about the **nitrogen cycle**:

a) Why is nitrogen essential for life?

b) How do

    i)   plants

    ii) animals

    obtain nitrogen?

c) Why does the nitrogen cycle work better in well aerated soil?

d) Why is soil made more fertile by growing peas, beans or clover?

e) If a farmer adds no fertiliser to the land, the crop yield will fall within a few years. However, a woodland has no added fertiliser, yet its production does not decline. Why should this be so?

f) In sewage treatment plants, the water containing sewage is often aerated. Why?

4 The bacteria involved in the **nitrogen cycle** are:

　　　　decay bacteria　　　nitrifying bacteria　　　nitrogen-fixing bacteria
　　　　denitrifying bacteria

a)　Copy the following diagram, which summarises the nitrogen cycle, and in the boxes write the names of the bacteria active at each stage:

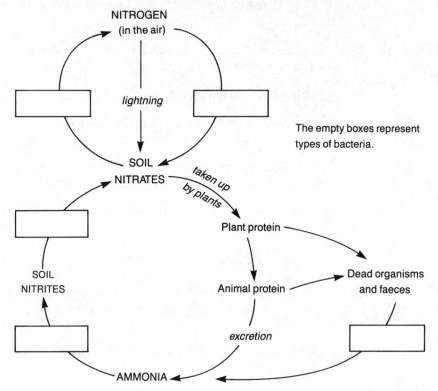

The empty boxes represent types of bacteria.

b)　In the nitrogen cycle, which of the bacteria are helpful and which are unhelpful?

2 Feeding Relationships

1 Each of the following lists of organisms shows the members of a **food chain**. In each list, arrange the organisms in their correct ecological order, starting with the plant (the producer).

a)　water-flea, stickleback, microscopic algae

b)　rose-bush, ladybird, greenfly

c)　fox, grass, rabbit

d)　snail, thrush, leaves

2 Copy and complete these sentences by choosing the correct words from inside the brackets:

a) A producer organism (makes food/eats other organisms/produces energy).

b) A consumer organism (makes food/eats other organisms/consumes light energy).

c) Producers are usually (animals/parasites/green plants).

d) A herbivore (eats plants/photosynthesises/eats other animals).

e) A carnivore (eats plants/photosynthesises/eats other animals).

f) The process by which the energy of sunlight is transferred to food is called (photosynthesis/respiration/symbiosis).

g) The process by which the energy is released from food is called (photosynthesis/respiration/symbiosis).

h) Microbes which feed on the dead bodies of animals and plants are called (parasites/decomposers/predators).

3 Consider this food chain and then answer the following questions:

   plant → greenfly → frog → snake

a) Which organism is the producer?

b) Which organisms are the primary, secondary and tertiary consumers?

c) Which organism is a herbivore?

d) Which organisms are carnivores?

e) Which organism is the top carnivore?

4 The following organisms can often be found living in the same habitat:

   caterpillar   earthworm   fox   greenfly   green plant   hawk
   ladybird   rabbit   small bird

a) Construct a **food web** of the habitat. Use arrows to show the direction in which the energy is passing through the food web.

b) Answer these questions about your food web:

   i) Which organism is the producer?

   ii) Name *two* organisms which are primary consumers.

   iii) Name *two* organisms which are secondary consumers.

   iv) Name an organism which is a herbivore.

   v) Name an organism which is a carnivore.

   vi) Which organism converts light energy into chemical energy?

   vii) What would be the possible consequences of a reduction in the number of rabbits?

5 This diagram represents the numbers of different organisms in a certain food chain:

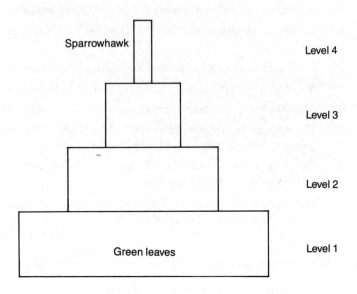

a)   What is this type of diagram called?

b)   Copy the diagram and suggest organisms which could be at levels 2 and 3.

6 After frequent visits to a pond near their school, and a long practical study, a class of pupils identified and observed many organisms. They gathered together the following information:

> Pond-snails feed on algae and pond-weed.
> Pond-skaters feed on water-fleas.
> Water-beetles feed on water-fleas and mayfly larvae.
> Roach feed on pond-snails, water-beetles and pond-skaters.
> Hydras feed on water-fleas.
> Mayfly larvae feed on algae.
> Water-fleas feed on algae.

a)   Construct a food web from this information.

b)   Name the producers in the food web.

c)   What happens to the animals and plants that die before being eaten by other animals?

d)   Draw a pyramid of numbers for the pond organisms and label each trophic level.

7 a) Copy the following pyramids of numbers and in each case choose the correct food chain which it represents. Write out the food chain below its pyramid.

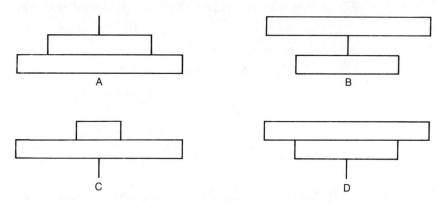

A

B

C

D

Food chains:

wheat → rat → flea   oak tree → aphid → bird

grass → rabbit → fox   cabbage → caterpillar → wasp parasite

b) What is 'biomass'?

c) Draw a pyramid of biomass for each of the examples B, C and D in the question above?

8 a) Copy and complete this paragraph about **energy flow**:

Food chains, webs and pyramids are ways of representing the flow of _____ through an ecosystem. The original source of energy is the _____. Green plants use this energy to manufacture _____ in the process of _____. This energy is incorporated into the body of the plant as it _____. The energy is transferred along a food chain to the _____. At each step in the chain energy is lost because each consumer _____ some of it for its own life processes. During the process of decay, the energy in dead bodies and excretory material is passed on to _____.

b) State *two* ways in which energy is lost along a food chain.

c) Explain why

i)   the number of organisms decreases at each trophic level in an ecosystem.

ii) the territories of top predators are usually very large.

iii) there are rarely more than five links in a food chain.

9 A knowledge of ecological pyramids is important in the production of food for humans.

a) Use the information given on the diagram below to calculate the percentage of food energy eaten by the bullock which is converted into beef.

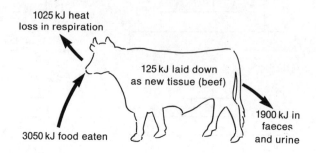

1025 kJ heat loss in respiration

125 kJ laid down as new tissue (beef)

1900 kJ in faeces and urine

3050 kJ food eaten

b) Why is the animal so inefficient at converting grass into beef?

c) Which of the following food chains is more efficient in providing food for Man? Explain your choice.

i)   grass → sheep → Man

ii) soya bean → Man.

d) Explain how the following farming methods improve production.

i)   The animals are kept indoors in a controlled environment.

ii)   Food is harvested and brought to them.

iii) Growth hormone and antibiotics are often given to the animals.

3 Where Do Organisms Live?

1 a) A **habitat** is a particular place where organisms live. Which of the places in the list below would you call a habitat?

aeroplane   cloud   field   hedgerow   litter-bin   pond
pebble   stream   statue   seashore   pavement   sun
motor car   rain   woodland   wind

b) Every habitat has certain conditions that make it suitable for some organisms to live in, but not others. Look at the following list of organisms and decide which of them would be found

i)   in a woodland   ii)   on the seashore   iii)   in a pond

stickleback   oak-tree   woodpecker   crab   ladybird
oyster-catcher   heron   water-lily   leaf-hopper   winkle
badger   seaweed   water-boatman   limpet   bluebell

c) The conditions in the habitat make up the **environment**.

   i) Decide which of the features in the list below are part of the **physical** environment and which are part of the **biological** environment. Record your answer in a table with these headings:

Physical environment	Biological environment

predators   temperature   light intensity   food supply   humidity
depth of water   saltiness of water   rainfall

   ii) Which of the above conditions are most important to a plant living in a wood?

d) **The organisms which live in a particular habitat are adapted to living there.**

   i) Copy the sentence above.

   ii) Explain the meaning of the word 'adapted'.

e) Look at the illustrations below and on the next page. Each one shows an organism in its natural habitat. Suggest *one* way in which each organism is adapted to living there.

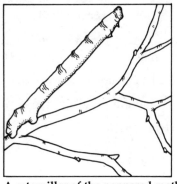

A caterpillar of the peppered moth

Seaweed

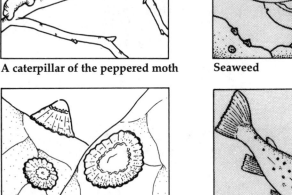

Limpets on a rocky shore

Fish

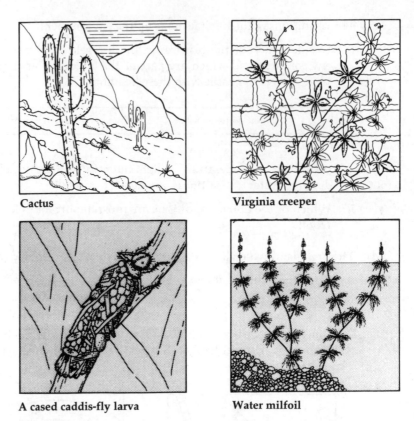

Cactus

Virginia creeper

A cased caddis-fly larva

Water milfoil

f) A **microhabitat** is a small part of a larger habitat, with a particular set of conditions. For example, a dead log in a wood is a microhabitat.

   i) Give another example of a microhabitat in a wood.

   ii) Give an example of a microhabitat in each of these habitats:

   stream   pond   rocky shore

2 The diagram below shows the layers in a wood.

1

2

3
4

a) Copy the diagram.

b) Which of the numbered regions corresponds to

   i)   the field (herb) layer?

   ii)   the canopy (tree) layer?

   iii) the shrub layer?

   iv) the ground layer?

c) Name one plant you would expect to find in *each* of the layers.

d) What effects will the canopy layer have on the conditions inside the wood in the summer?

e) Explain why woodland plants which grow and flower early in spring often have bulbs.

3 a) The diagram below shows a vertical section through a piece of apparatus which can be used to investigate the conditions wood-lice prefer.

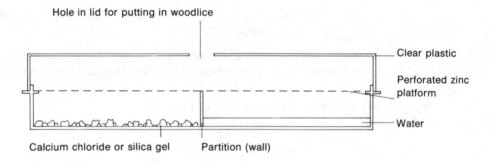

Hole in lid for putting in woodlice

Clear plastic

Perforated zinc platform

Water

Calcium chloride or silica gel   Partition (wall)

   i)   What is the name of this apparatus?

   ii)   What is the function of the calcium chloride or silica gel?

b) Ten wood-lice were placed in the apparatus, and the number of wood-lice in each half was counted every minute for six minutes. The results are shown in the table below.

Time (minutes)	Number of wood-lice in left-hand side	Number of wood-lice in right-hand side
1	4	6
2	2	8
3	1	9
4	2	8
5	1	9
6	1	9

i)   Plot both sets of results on one graph, clearly labelling which curve is
      which. Label the axes as shown.

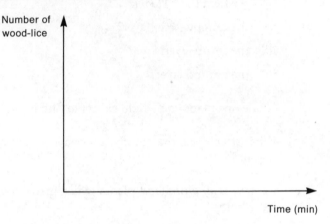

Number of
wood-lice

Time (min)

ii)   Which conditions do the wood-lice prefer?

iii)   When the passage between the two sides of the apparatus was blocked,
       the wood-lice in the dry side were bunched up together against the sides.
       How does this behaviour help the wood-lice to survive?

c) i)   Describe how you could use the same apparatus to see if wood-lice prefer
          dark or light conditions.

    ii)   When such an experiment was carried out, it was found that wood-lice
          preferred the dark conditions. How does this help them to survive?

4 The diagram below shows a pitfall trap.

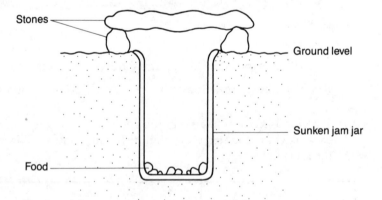

Stones

Ground level

Sunken jam jar

Food

a) What types of animals would you expect to collect in this kind of trap?

b) Explain how you would use the trap to investigate

    i)   whether a particular animal is more active on the forest floor at night
          than during the day

    ii)   the sort of food beetles prefer

5 Read the following passage and then answer the questions that follow:

> An area of poor agricultural land which had always been used for rough grazing of sheep during summer was to be 'improved' by ploughing and sowing with good grazing grasses. Conservationists opposed the change on two grounds: firstly that the area was of special scientific interest because of the rare heathland plants and animals; secondly because they said that the mixture of flowers indicated a soil of low mineral content, making it of little use for farming.
>
> A group of scientists surveyed the area. Firstly they sampled the vegetation using quadrats, and then made a line transect from the poor agricultural grazing through to previously 'improved' grassland. The invertebrates and vertebrates were sampled throughout the area. Lastly numerous soil samples were taken and tested.
>
> The final report sent in by the scientists indicated that the variety of flowers was good and that the variety of animals was also good, the level of soil minerals was low, but that the 'improved' grassland yielded good grazing, superior in quality to the rough grazing.

a) Why did the farmer want to improve the grassland?

b) i) Suggest two reasons why ploughing might 'improve' the grassland.

    ii) Suggest two other ways in which the farmer might 'improve' his grassland.

c) Why did the conservationists oppose the change?

d) i) What is a quadrat?

    ii) Explain how quadrats could be used to survey the vegetation.

    iii) List the main reasons for obtaining inaccurate results when using a quadrat.

e) i) Explain how the scientists would have made the line transect.

    ii) What do you think the line transect was used to show?

f) i) Suggest two ways in which the invertebrates might be sampled.

    ii) Suggest two ways in which the vertebrates might be sampled.

6 Each of the words in the following list is defined below. Write out each of the definitions matched with the correct word from the list.

> ecology   community   habitat   population   microhabitat
> environment

a) The study of living things in relation to their environment.

b) A particular place where an organism lives.

c) The conditions, physical and biological, that are present in the place where an organism lives.

d) The living organisms of different species which live in a particular habitat.

e) A particular place within a habitat, with conditions to which certain organisms are adapted.

f)   The number of individuals of a species that live in a particular habitat.

7 The diagram below shows a section through a pond where two samples of animals, sample A and sample B, were collected.

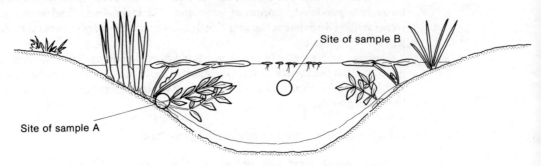

Site of sample B

Site of sample A

The table shows the animals collected in each sample.

Animal	Number of animals	
	Sample A	Sample B
Snails	90	2
Mites	140	80
Leeches	5	2
True worms	80	0
Flatworms	10	1
Insects – Damselfly nymphs	30	5
Water boatmen	170	45
Mayfly nymphs	50	100
Midge larvae	120	35
Beetles	30	15

a) How would you collect the animals at each site in order to make a fair comparison of population size?

b) i) Which animal was present in the largest number at site A?

ii) Which animal was present in the largest number in the combined samples, A and B?

c) Draw a pie chart to show the numbers of **insects** in sample A. (It may help to divide the circle into 20 equal sectors.)

d) Suggest *two* reasons for the difference in number of worms between sample A and sample B.

4 The Study of a Habitat – an Ecological Survey

1 Name a habitat you have studied. Describe exactly where this habitat was.

2 Draw a sketch map of the particular area you studied.

3 What physical conditions of the environment might control where organisms live in your habitat?

4 List the organisms that you found in your habitat under three separate headings:

Producers	Herbivores	Carnivores

5 a) Draw *three* simple food chains from your habitat.

b) Draw a simple food web from your habitat.

6 a) Name *three* animals that you have found in your habitat.

b) For each of the animals you have named give the following information:

i) How did you catch the animal?

ii) Where in the habitat did you find it?

iii) What features of the animal enabled you to identify it?

iv) How is the animal adapted to living in this habitat?

7 a) Name one organism whose distribution was found to be uneven in your habitat. Describe its distribution.

b) Describe how you investigated the distribution of this organism.

c) What environmental condition or conditions may control the distribution of this organism?

8 During the year there will be changes in the organisms within your habitat. Write down *one* change that occurs in each of *three* named organisms. Present the information in a table as follows:

Organism	Change that occurs	Time of year
1. 2. 3.		

9 Suggest a problem faced by *one* named organism from your habitat and explain how it overcomes this problem.

10 a) What is meant by 'succession'?

b) Describe *two* changes that have occurred in your habitat as a result of succession.

c) What is the climax community?

5 Changes Through the Year

1 Complete these two sentences, choosing only the correct word or words from inside the brackets:

a) Deciduous trees (do/do not) lose their leaves in autumn.

b) Evergreen trees (do/do not) lose their leaves in autumn.

2 Which trees in this list are deciduous and which are evergreen?

oak   fir   ash   sycamore   spruce   horse-chestnut   holly
cedar   beech

3 a) Look at the trees in the area where you live. Try to identify them.

b) Give *two* examples each of trees in your area which are

i) deciduous

ii) evergreen

c) What visible characteristic of the trees you have named enabled you to identify them?

4 a) Copy the diagram below of a horse-chestnut twig in winter. Replace the letters A–F with labels from this list:

> **lateral bud**   **terminal bud**   **bud scales**   **lenticels**   **leaf scar**
> **girdle scar (scale scar)**

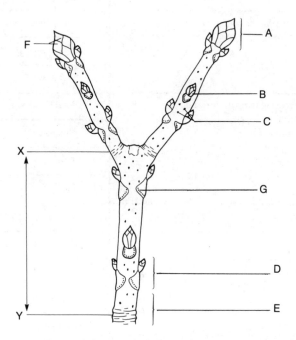

b) What caused the marks labelled G?

c) What causes the girdle or scale scar?

d) How old is the piece of wood on the diagram between X and Y?

e) What will happen to the part labelled A in the spring?

5 The environment in a particular habitat does not always stay the same. The seasons and the weather change, altering the conditions for life. These changes are often so predictable that many organisms have a pattern of behaviour which matches them. Winter always follows summer, night always follows day. Organisms may behave in different ways at different times of day or year as conditions change.

a) In what ways will the physical conditions change in a rock pool during the day?

b) In what ways will the physical conditions change in a deciduous woodland during a year?

c) Copy and complete the table below to show how some organisms respond to regular changes in the environment.

Environmental change	Organism	Behavioural response
Decreasing temperature and/or decreasing day length	Hedgehog	
	Oak-tree	
	Swallow	
Increasing temperature and/or lengthening days	Seeds	
	Bluebell	
	Robin	
	Bat	
Incoming tide	Limpet	
Ebbing tide	Oyster-catcher	
Dawn	Blackbird	
	Dandelion	
	Badger	
Nightfall	Bat	
	Owl	
	Moth	

d) Many animals produce young only in the spring. What are the advantages of this?

6 a) How does the bark of a tree help it to survive the winter?

b) Why is it an advantage for a tree to be deciduous?

c) How do the following evergreen trees reduce the amount of water lost by evaporation from their leaves?

i) holly

ii) pine

7 Imagine that you walked through a wood (or a group of trees in a park) in May and then again in December. Make a list of the differences you would notice at the two times of year. Use a table to present the information:

May	December

6 Adaptation and Survival

1 Copy the table below. It shows three adaptations that help the common frog to survive in its habitat.

Organism	Adaptation	Survival value
Common frog	1. Webbed feet and large hind limbs	Quick, strong swimmer, can escape predators
	2. Eyes and nostrils on the top of its head	It can remain mostly hidden under water, whilst breathing and watching for food and predators.
	3. Sticky tongue	Catching food

Now copy the following tables, and complete them by filling in the spaces in the third column:

Organism	Adaptation	Survival value
Earthworm	1. Soft slimy skin	
	2. Bristles	
	3. Moves away from light	

Organism	Adaptation	Survival value
Tapeworm	1. Hooks and suckers on the head 2. Each segment contains both male and female sex organs 3. Produces millions of eggs	

Organism	Adaptation	Survival value
Desert cactus	1. Leaves reduced to spines 2. Thick swollen stem 3. Very long roots	

Organism	Adaptation	Survival value
Camel	1. Broad feet 2. Fat is concentrated in the hump on its back 3. Body cells can tolerate severe water loss	

Organism	Adaptation	Survival value
Water milfoil (a pond weed)	1. Long floppy stem 2. Leaves only present at the surface of the water 3. Flowers formed above the surface of the pond	

Organism	Adaptation	Survival value
Bony fish	1. Gills 2. Streamlined shape 3. Swim-bladder	

Organism	Adaptation	Survival value
Woodpecker	1. Short strong fan-tail feathers 2. Long tongue with sharp tip 3. Pointed, chisel-like beak	

Organism	Adaptation	Survival value
Elephant	1. Large ears 2. Very little hair 3. Wide legs like tree-trunks	

Organism	Adaptation	Survival value
Polar bear	1. Large body 2. Small ears 3. Thick subcutaneous fat layer	

2 Explain the following observations.

a) The pigmy shrew is Britain's smallest mammal. It is only about 10 cm long including its tail. It can only survive in southern England.

b) Baby penguins and seals have thick fluffy coats, but the adults do not.

c) Humming birds are the smallest birds in the world. They feed on nectar and can only live in tropical countries.

d) Newborn babies need to be kept very warm. Many have died in cold bedrooms.

e) Penguins huddle together during the Antarctic winter, changing places with one another from time to time. During the winter, honey bees do the same in their hives.

f) When the tropical day is at its hottest, elephants will often stand in the shade with their huge ears spread out.

7 The Soil

1 Pair these groups of words to form sentences:

a) **Soil is formed from rock**   in colour than subsoil.

b) **Weathering agents include**   remains of dead organisms, called humus.

c) **Topsoil is generally darker**   important for plant growth.

d)   Topsoil contains decaying   rain, wind, snow and frost.

e)   If a sample of soil is shaken in   gravel, humus, mineral salts, water
water and allowed to stand   and air.

f)   The finest particles of soil are   by the action of weathering agents.

g)   Soil contains sand, clay,   nitrogen, phosphorus, potassium
and magnesium.

h)   Mineral salts in soil water are   filled with air and water.

i)   Some important elements in   clay particles with a diameter less
mineral salts are   than 0.002 mm.

j)   Spaces between the soil particles   the larger particles settle first.
are

2   A sample of soil was placed in a tall glass measuring cylinder with a large volume
of water. It was then shaken and left to settle completely. The results are shown in
this diagram:

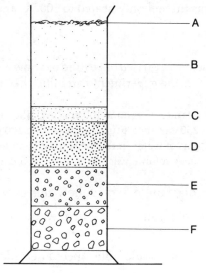

a)   Copy the diagram and replace the letters A–F with correct labels.

b)   Which soil particles settle first and why?

c)   Why does part B appear cloudy?

3   Explain the importance of the following components of the soil:

a)   humus   d)   soil water

b)   lime   e)   soil air

c)   mineral salts

4 An experiment was carried out to find the amount of water in a sample of soil. The sample was weighed, and heated at 100 °C until a constant mass (weight) was obtained. The results were as follows:

Mass of container	20.0 g
Mass of container and soil	45.0 g
Mass of container and soil after heating for ten minutes	41.5 g
Mass of container and soil after heating for twenty minutes	40.0 g
Mass of container and soil after heating for thirty minutes	40.0 g

a) What was the original mass of the soil, before heating?

b) What was the mass of water in the original soil sample?

c) The percentage of water in the original sample of soil can be worked out like this:

$$\frac{\text{mass of water}}{\text{mass of original soil sample}} \times 100$$

What was the percentage of water in the original soil sample?

d) Why was the soil heated for thirty minutes rather than just twenty minutes?

e) Why was the soil only heated to 100 °C and not to a higher temperature?

5 An experiment was carried out to find out how much air was in a sample of soil. Read this account of the experiment carefully, then answer the questions.

> A container of volume 100 cm³ was filled with soil. 100 cm³ of water was placed in a 250 cm³ measuring cylinder. The 100 cm³ of soil was carefully added to the 100 cm³ of water in the measuring cylinder, and the new volume was recorded. The new volume was found to be 155 cm³.

a) Draw a diagram to explain how this experiment was carried out.

b) What would you have noticed on the surface of the water as the soil was added?

c) What volume would you expect after adding 100 cm³ of soil to 100 cm³ of water?

d) What is the difference between the expected volume and the actual volume after the soil was added?

e) What caused this difference?

f) What was the percentage of air in this soil sample?

$$\left(\frac{\text{volume of air}}{\text{volume of soil (100 cm}^3)} \times 100\right)$$

g) In a good soil, the percentage of air is 25. Why does an experiment such as this one not give an accurate result?

6 Earthworms live in the soil. Describe *four* ways in which the earthworm is useful to gardeners.

7 The apparatus shown below can be used to extract small animals from a sample of soil.

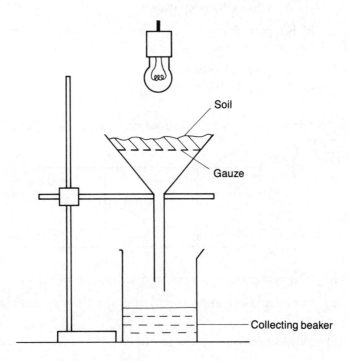

a) Draw and label the apparatus.

b) What *two* effects will the lamp have on the soil?

c) How do soil animals respond to the effect of the lamp?

d) Why should the lamp not be placed too close to the surface of the soil?

8 Below are seven pairs of statements about soil. Construct a table with two headings:

Sandy soil	Clay soil

For each pair of descriptions below, decide which one applies to sandy soil and which one to clay soil; then complete the table.

a) Composed mainly of large particles
   Composed mainly of fine particles

b) Contains large air spaces
Contains small air spaces

c) Poorly drained and aerated
Well drained and aerated

d) Useful chemicals are washed out when it rains
Holds on to useful chemicals well

e) Rich in plant food
Poor in plant food

f) Loose, light and easy to dig
Cold, heavy and difficult to dig

9 An analysis of two soil samples carried out by a gardener gave the following results:

	Sample A	Sample B
Sand	85%	22%
Clay	14%	70%
Humus	1%	8%

a) Give *one* advantage and *one* disadvantage of each soil sample.

b) How could you improve soil from sample A so that plants would grow better in it?

c) How could you improve soil of type B?

d) The ideal garden soil is called **loam**.

   i) What, roughly, should its composition be?
   ii) Why is loam better for plant growth than sandy or clay soil?

e) i) Why is peaty soil not very fertile?
   ii) Why is it improved by adding lime?

f) Why is chalky soil alkaline?

10 There are living organisms in the soil which are too small to be seen with the naked eye or even a hand-lens.

a) Name *two* different groups of such organisms.

b) What do they feed on?

c) What benefit are these micro-organisms to larger plants growing in the soil?

d) Give a detailed account, with diagrams, of how you would set up an experiment to show that these micro-organisms are present in soil. Point out any controls you would need, and describe the results you would expect.

11 Three different soil samples of equal volume were placed in plugged glass funnels, as shown in the diagram. Equal volumes of water were poured at the same time on to each soil sample. Records were kept of the time taken for 2 cm³ of water to drip through and the results are shown in the table below.

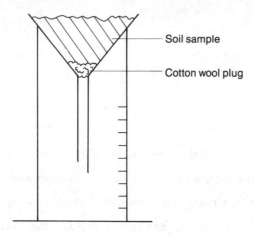

Sample	A	B	C
Time	45 seconds	10 seconds	7.5 minutes

a) Which of these soil samples is likely to contain the most sand? Give a reason for your answer.

b) Which of the soils is likely to contain the most clay? Give a reason for your answer.

12 A glass tube was plugged at one end with gauze and was then filled with dry sand. A similar tube was set up containing dry clay. Each tube was then clamped with the gauze end in a beaker of water. The side of each tube was marked at regular intervals of time to show the level of water inside it. These results were recorded in the form of a table shown below.

Time (hours)	Height reached by water (cm)	
	Clay	Sand
6	4	20
11	9	24
18	17	26
24	25	28
30	31	28
36	36	28
42	40	28
48	45	28
54	46	28
60	46	28

a) Draw a diagram of the apparatus.

b) Use the results to plot two graphs on the same axes. Label the axes as shown.

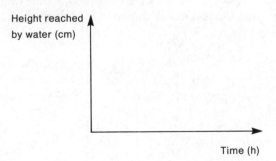

c) How long did the water in the column of clay take to reach a height of 35 cm?

d) In which sample did the water rise more quickly at first?

e) After how many hours were the two water levels the same?

f) If, after 60 hours, the beakers of water had been removed from beneath the tubes which type of soil would have lost its water in the shortest time?

8 Decay

1 a) What types of microbe are known as decomposers? What do they do?

b) What would happen to the bodies of dead animals and plants if there were no decomposers?

2 a) Construct a table to show **the conditions required for decay to occur.** Your table should look like this:

Conditions required	Reason
1. 2. 3. 4.	

b) Explain why

i)   extinct mammoths have been found undecayed in Siberia.

ii) the bodies of Egyptian kings have been found undecayed in the pyramids.

iii) biologists keep specimens of animals and plants in alcohol.

3 An experiment was set up as shown below.

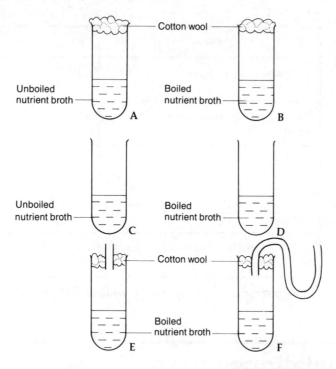

a) In which of the tubes would the broth go cloudy? Give reasons for your choices.

b) What difference would you expect in the results of tubes D and E?

c) Explain the different results in tubes E and F.

4 a) Choose words from the list below to complete the following sentences about **decay**.

  atmosphere   carbon dioxide   microbes   nitrogen   plants
  simpler   soil   water

  i)   Dead bodies are decayed by _____ .

  ii)   During decay complex chemicals are broken down into _____ ones.

  iii) Carbohydrates are broken down into _____ and _____ .

  iv)   Proteins are broken down into _____ salts.

  v)   The simple substances can be absorbed and used by _____ .

  vi)   The process of decay puts back into the _____ and _____ the chemicals that plants take out.

  b) i)   Explain why manure and compost are good for plant growth.

   ii)   Why must fertiliser be applied to soil which has been used to grow crops?

5 a) Below are some rules for making a **compost heap**. Copy and complete the table.

Rules	Reason
The compost heap should be sheltered from wind and sun.	
Only biodegradable material should be added.	
A thin layer of soil should be added occasionally.	
The compost should be kept moist but not saturated.	
The heap should be turned with a fork from time to time.	

b) Name *three* groups of organisms which will help in the decay process.

9 Populations

1 How do single-celled organisms such as protists and bacteria reproduce?

2 A single bacterium is capable of dividing once every 20 minutes in 'good' conditions.

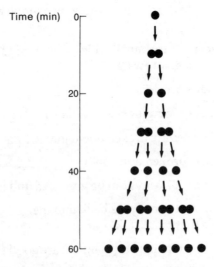

a) What would be 'good' conditions for bacteria to grow in?

   b)   Starting with a single bacterium, how many bacteria would there be after

   i)   one hour?

   ii)   two hours?

   iii)   three hours?

3 The **growth rate** of an aerobic bacterium was measured by inoculating some cells into a sterile nutrient broth kept at 25 °C. At the times given below, a 1 ml (cm^3) sample was withdrawn and the number of living cells in the sample was determined. The results are shown below:

Hours after inoculation	Number of living cells (millions per 1 ml (cm³))
0	10
5	10
10	50
15	410
20	450
25	460
30	200
50	50

   a)   Plot these results.

   b)   Label the following parts of your graph:
      A – Growth rate of the population is very slow.
      B – Growth rate of the population is very rapid.
      C – Growth rate of the population is fairly constant.
      D – Growth rate is declining rapidly.

   c)   Account for the shape of the graph by completing the following table:

	A	B	C	D
Rate at which cells are being produced		very fast		
Rate at which cells are dying				very fast
Amount of food and oxygen available	high concentration			
Build-up of toxic excretory products		low concentration		

   d)   Calculate the maximum rate of increase in cells per hour.

e) How might the results have been different if

    i)   the culture had been maintained at 15 °C instead of 25 °C?

    ii)   the culture had been maintained in nitrogen instead of air?

    iii) another microorganism having the same nutritional requirements had also been introduced into the broth?

4 a) Study the two **population pyramids** below.

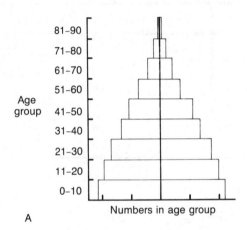

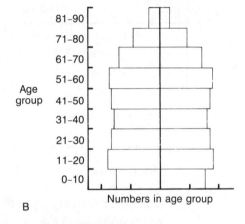

A

An increasing population

The population will increase if all the organisms in the younger age groups grow up and reproduce

B

A stable population

This population should not change much in size as the sizes of the younger age groups are only slightly larger than the older ones

Copy the following paragraphs, choosing the correct word or words from inside the brackets to complete them.

Population pyramid A is typical of a (developed/developing) country for example (Brazil/Great Britain). There is a (high/low) birth rate and a (high/low) death rate. There are proportionally more (young/old) people and as they (reproduce/die) the population will continue to (increase/decrease).

Population pyramid B is typical of a (developed/developing) country for example (Brazil/Great Britain). The shape of the pyramid is more like (an arrow/a pillar). The standard of living appears to be (higher/lower) because the population pyramid shows that more people (live longer/die sooner). The birth rate is (high/low). Populations like this (increase continually/remain fairly stable).

b) Name *three* fatal diseases which may be suffered by people represented by:

    i) pyramid A

    ii) pyramid B

5 The table below gives the **world human population** at various times since 1650.

Year AD	Approximate world population (millions)
1650	500
1850	1000
1900	1500
1925	2000
1950	2500
1960	3000
1975	4000
2000	?

a) Plot these data on graph paper, putting 'Year AD' on the horizontal axis beginning at 1600 and 'Number of people' on the vertical axis. Include the year 2000 on your time scale.

b) What would you predict to be the world human population in the year AD 2000?

c) How many years did it take the population to increase from

   i) 1000 million to 2000 million?

   ii) 2000 million to 3000 million?

   iii) 3000 million to 4000 million?

d) Make a list of the factors that normally stop animal populations from growing indefinitely.

e) For each of these factors, suggest a reason why it has failed to control the human population.

f) Write a short essay about the effects that the increasing human population has on the earth. Include comments on food, resources, pollution, wildlife, crime and living-space.

g) Why do you think the populations of developed countries, e.g. USA and Western Europe, are levelling off, whereas those of developing countries are continuing to rise at a very fast rate?

6 The graph overleaf shows **changes in population numbers** of snowshoe hares and lynx over eighty years in Northern Canada. Study the graph carefully and then answer the following questions.

a) How many hares were there in 1885?

b) How many lynx were there in 1885?

c) i) Suggest what hares eat.

   ii) Suggest what lynx eat.

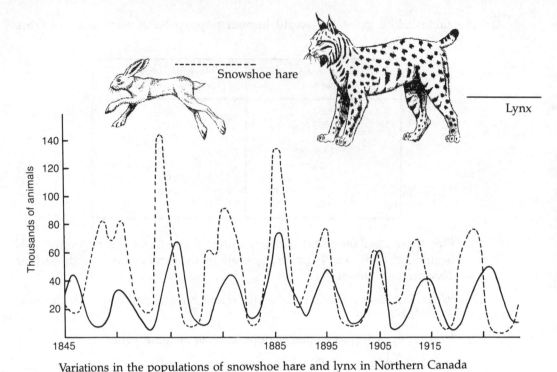

Variations in the populations of snowshoe hare and lynx in Northern Canada

d)   What happened to the numbers of lynx as the hare population increased? Explain your observation.

e)   What effect did large numbers of lynx have on the hare population? Explain your observation.

f)   What happened to the numbers of lynx as the hare population fell?

g)   How might this information on the changing populations of hares and lynx in Northern Canada have been collected?

h)   What does this information tell you about the relationship between a predator and its prey?

10 People and the Environment

1   What is a **pest**? Make a list of *ten* organisms that people consider to be pests, and explain why each one is either harmful or a nuisance.

2   Explain the following words:

pesticides   insecticides   fungicides   herbicides

3 Read this passage about **biological control** and then answer the questions.

> In the 1860s the orange orchards of California were threatened by an insect pest which had been accidentally introduced from Australia. All the insecticides known then were useless against the insects because these had a wax-like cuticle which was resistant to sprays. It was eventually found that in Australia the number of these insects was kept down by a small species of ladybird. The Australian ladybirds were released into the American orange orchards and within two years the insects had been brought under control and the orange orchards were saved.

a) Why did the insect become a pest in California?

b) Why was it not a pest in Australia?

c) Why could the insect not be controlled by insecticides in the 1860s?

d) How was the insect finally brought under control?

e) Suggest why the pest has recently reappeared.

f) What is the advantage of using biological control?

g) What are the possible problems of using biological control?

h) Give *two* other examples of humans using biological control to keep down a pest.

4 Read this passage about **modern farming methods** and then answer the questions:

> Any expensive piece of farm machinery is only a profitable investment if it is constantly in use. Farms have become larger and hedges have been ripped up. Many farmers do not keep cattle and so have no farmyard manure. Large amounts of chemical fertilisers have to be used. This has the effect of making some soils thin and dusty, particularly when cereals are grown year after year. When the weather is wet, such soils become infertile and waterlogged. In dry and windy conditions the soil blows away in dust storms.

a) What is meant by 'a profitable investment'?

b) Name an 'expensive piece of farm machinery'.

c) Why do you think that many farmers do not keep cattle?

d) Suggest *two* advantages and *two* disadvantages of using

    i)   farmyard manure

    ii)   chemical fertilisers

e) How can cereal farmers reduce the effects of artificial fertilisers on the soil?

f) Why is it necessary to grow crops such as wheat in very large quantities?

g) What is monoculture? Suggest two reasons why crops are grown in this way.

5 Read the following account of an experiment and then answer the questions:

Flies were sprayed with insecticide and some died. The survivors were counted and then allowed to breed. The next generation was sprayed with an insecticide. The survivors were again counted and then allowed to breed. The experiment was repeated for eight generations and the results recorded in the bar graph below.

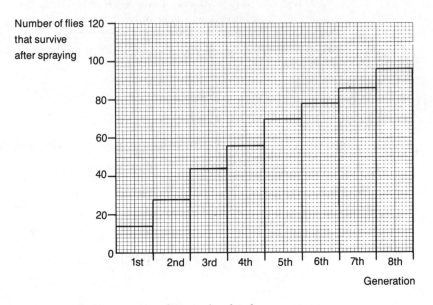

a) How many flies were alive during the third generation?

b) What do you notice about the number of flies that survive each spraying?

c) Give a reason for your answer to part b).

d) Give *two* reasons why the use of insecticides is not the best way of destroying pests.

e) What is the difference between a general and a specific insecticide?

6 The following table compares the total hedge length dug up by farmers during the period 1945–72, in five English counties. Study the table and then answer the questions.

County	Percentage of hedge removed	Main agricultural activity
Huntingdonshire	38	crops
Dorset	10	dairy
Herefordshire	10	mixed
Yorkshire	15	crops
Warwickshire	7	dairy, mixed

a) Suggest reasons why more hedges have been removed in Huntingdonshire and Yorkshire.

b)   Suggest *two* reasons why hedges might be useful to farmers.

c)   Why are hedges useful to wild animals?

d)   Why does growing crops in small fields reduce the effect of pests?

e)   Why is it better to space out the plants in a field?

f)   Many farmers now leave a corner of a field uncultivated. What do they hope to gain by doing this?

g)   Suggest *three* ways in which modern farming has harmed wildlife.

h)   Explain how the removal of one animal from a food chain or web can upset the balance of nature in a community.

7   In an attempt to get rid of a type of mosquito infesting a lake, the authorities sprayed the lake with DDT. This appeared to be successful, since the mosquitoes died while other animals and plants seemed to be little affected. Consequently the treatment was repeated the next year. Some years later many large fish-eating birds were found to be dead or dying. When their bodies were analysed they were found to contain large amounts of DDT. Other animals and plants were examined and the results are shown in the table.

Organisms	Amount of DDT per unit mass
Small fish	10 units
Animal plankton	5 units
Plant plankton	1 unit
Large fish	100 units
Lake water	0.3 units
Grebes (fish-eating birds)	1600 units

a)   Draw a food chain for the lake.

b)   Why was such a high dosage of DDT found in grebes?

c)   Why is DDT known as a persistent pesticide?

8   Look for an example of **pollution** in the area where you live.

a)   Say exactly where you found the pollution.

b)   What caused the pollution? Say what the pollutant was, and describe the source of it (where it came from).

c)   What are the effects of this pollution on

i)   the environment?

ii)   plants and animals (including humans)?

9 The diagram below shows freshwater animals associated with organic pollution. Study the diagram and answer the questions.

a) What happens to the concentration of oxygen in the water as sewage enters the river?

b) Which of the organisms shown can only survive in very polluted water?

c) Which organisms can only survive in very clean water?

d) What is a 'pollution-indicator organism'?

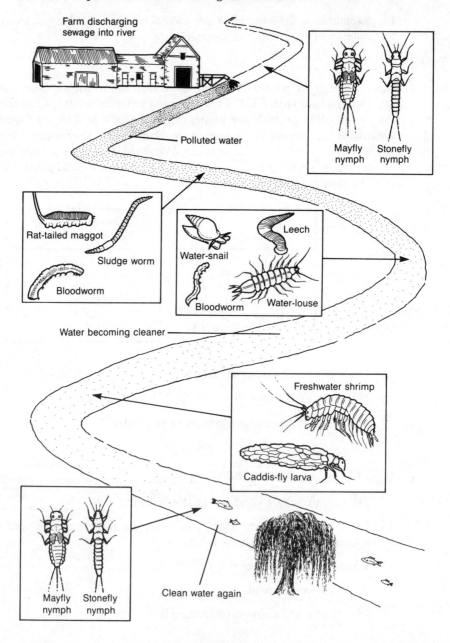

10 Cockshoot Broad is a lake in Norfolk. The map below shows that water flows into Cockshoot Broad from the River Bure. The area is surrounded by farmland that slopes down to the lake.

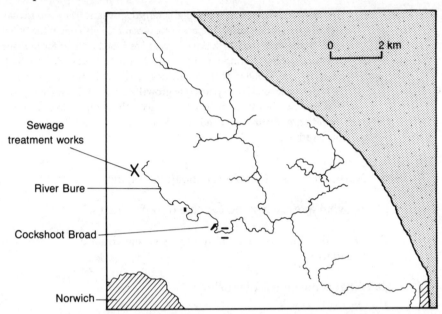

In recent years there has been a large increase in the levels of phosphate and nitrate in the waters of Cockshoot Broad.

a) Suggest where these chemicals could have come from.

b) When high levels of nitrate and phosphate pollute a lake or river, a series of changes takes place in the water, resulting in the death of many fish.
    Rewrite the following sentences in the correct order to give a summary of the changes which occur.

Nitrates and phosphates provide essential minerals for the growth of microscopic algae.

Populations of bacteria increase and use up large amounts of oxygen.

Nitrates and phosphates pollute the water.

Oxygen levels in the water drop sharply.

The water becomes green and cloudy as the numbers of algae rise.

Fish die due to lack of oxygen.

Many algae then die and provide food for decay bacteria.

c) Why is there a build-up of dead organic matter on the bottom of polluted lakes and rivers?

d) In some regions the level of nitrates in drinking water has increased. Why does this give cause for concern?

11 Read the passage which is about **herring fishing** and answer the questions which follow.

> The natural life span of a herring is ten to 15 years. They are sexually mature at the age of five years. During the breeding season shoals containing 500 million fish were once common in the North Sea. Herring are fished as food for humans. The traditional way of catching herring was by using drift nets. Whilst this method was being used there was no problem with overfishing. The numbers of herring caught in the North Sea each year could be replaced by growth. In the 1950s new methods of purse-seining and mid-depth fast trawling were started. These methods can catch complete shoals, including immature fish, and this led to a very large fall in the herring population of the North sea.

a) Name *one* breeding area for shoaling herring.

b) At what age are herring capable of reproducing?

c) Why did the use of drift nets not cause drastic reductions in the herring population?

d) What is meant by 'overfishing'?

e) Why is it important not to catch immature herring?

f) Name *two* fishing methods which have led to overfishing. Try to find out more about them.

g) Why has the human demand for fish increased so much over the last 100 years?

12 The diagram on the next page shows some of the components of an **Antarctic food web**.

a) i)   What is the ultimate source of energy for all the organisms in this food web?

   ii) Write out from this food web a food chain which involves *five* organisms.

   iii) From this food chain, name
        the producer
        one primary consumer
        one vertebrate carnivore.

   iv) From the diagram explain *two* ways in which human activities could reduce the blue whale population in Antarctica.

b) i)   It has been estimated that 4 million (4×10^6) square kilometres of Antarctic ocean contain up to 70 million (7×10^7) tonnes of krill. If the krill population covers 36 million (3.6×10^7) square kilometres of ocean in summer, what is its total biomass at this time? Show your working.

ii) Will the biomass of the phytoplankton be greater or smaller than the biomass of krill? Explain your answer.

iii) In winter much of the ocean where the krill live becomes covered with ice and very little light penetrates. Explain how this could cause a reduction in the krill population.

c) Explain, as fully as possible, what will happen to the bodies of the dead organisms which fall to the sea bed.

d) Both grey-headed and black-browed albatrosses feed on krill and squid. The black-browed albatross feeds almost entirely on krill whereas half of the food of the grey-headed albatross is squid. The squid population is the more stable from year to year.

Which of the two species of albatross is likely to produce more chicks over a period of several years? Explain your answer.

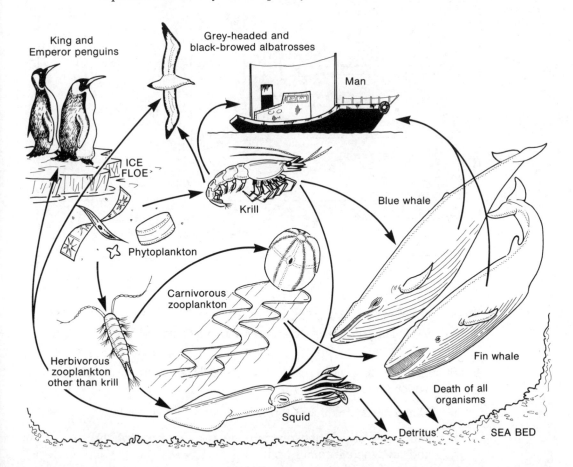

King and Emperor penguins

Grey-headed and black-browed albatrosses

Man

ICE FLOE

Krill

Blue whale

Phytoplankton

Carnivorous zooplankton

Herbivorous zooplankton other than krill

Fin whale

Death of all organisms

Squid

Detritus   SEA BED

13 The diagram below supplies information about the sensitivity of some aquatic organisms to the pH of water.

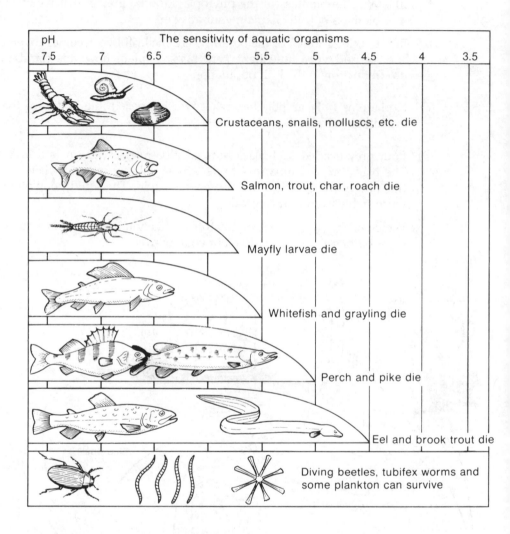

a)   i)   What is the pH of water below which perch and pike cannot live?

ii)   Which organisms are tolerant of the most acid water?

b) Sulphur dioxide gas can react with other substances in the air producing an acid which lowers the pH of rain.

i)   Name the acid which is formed.

ii)   Name one other atmospheric pollutant which contributes to acid rain and say where it comes from.

This diagram shows a map of **acid rain** in western Europe.

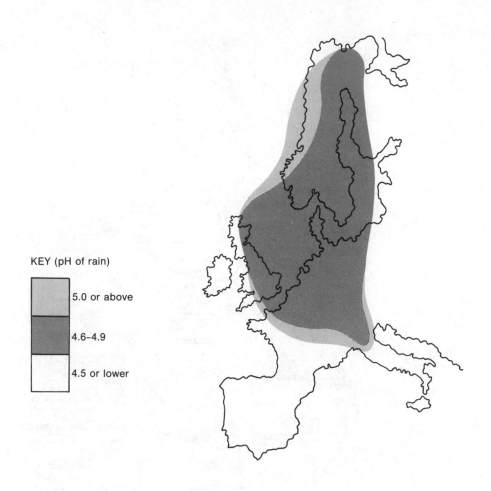

KEY (pH of rain)

5.0 or above

4.6–4.9

4.5 or lower

c) Explain why the pH of the rain falling on Ireland is different from that falling on northern Europe.

d) In Sweden over 9000 lakes no longer contain live fish. Some of the lakes have become 100 times more acidic in the past 50 years.

   Explain how this situation may have come about.

e) Most of the sulphur dioxide produced by coal-fired power stations could be removed by absorbing it using 'desulphurisation' equipment. Why is this *not* yet done on a large scale?

f) State *two* other ways in which this form of pollution could be reduced.

g) What effect do the pollutants in smoke have on our health?

14 Consider the motor vehicle:

a) What effect do motor vehicles have on our environment? Before you answer
    this question think about the following:

    the roads required to carry traffic   **traffic noise and vibration**
    the effect on the countryside of beauty spots easily reached by road
    the effect on human life

b) Over three million vehicles crowd into Los Angeles each day. What effect does
    this have on the atmosphere, and why?

c) How do motorway planners try to reduce the effects of these roads on the
    environment?

d) How can pollution by motor cars be reduced?

15 a) What do we mean by 'conservation' when referring to our environment?

b) Try to find out the names of at least two organisations concerned with conservation in Britain.

c) What is a nature reserve?

d) Try also to find the names of
   i) two plants
   ii) two birds
   iii) two other vertebrates

   that are protected by law in Britain. Why are they protected?

e) Why is it important not to pick wild flowers in the countryside?

f) What is a National Park? On the map of England and Wales, National Parks have been shaded in, and numbered A–J. Identify as many as you can.

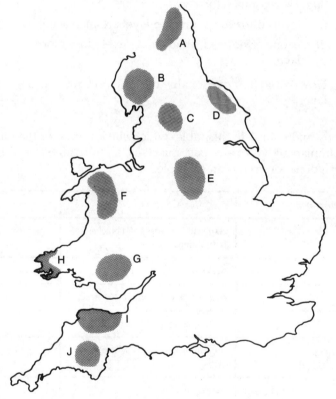

16 Read the passage below about the **ozone layer** and answer the questions which follow.

Ozone is a form of oxygen which has three atoms per molecule. It occurs naturally in the upper atmosphere, where the ozone layer blocks most of the harmful ultraviolet radiation from the Sun. At ground level, ozone can be produced as a result of reactions between pollutants from car exhaust fumes and atmospheric gases. Low-level ozone is itself a pollutant, which can cause damage to trees and animals. It is a very reactive gas.

Recently, studies by scientists have shown that, while levels of ozone at ground level are increasing, the amount of ozone in the upper atmosphere is dropping. One factor which is thought to be partly responsible for this drop in ozone is the widespread use of chemicals called CFCs (chlorofluorocarbons). Following release into the atmosphere, CFCs break down and release chlorine, which reacts with ozone in the upper atmosphere.

In September 1987, the U.K. government signed the Montreal Protocol, agreeing to reduce the use of CFCs by 50% by the end of the century. Some scientists believe that this will not be enough to prevent large-scale damage to life on Earth.

a) Give three common uses of CFCs.

b) Suggest one other source of atmospheric chlorine apart from CFCs.

c) Describe one possible consequence for humans of increased exposure to harmful ultraviolet radiation.

d) Suggest reasons why

    i)   levels of ozone at ground level are increasing

    ii)   ozone produced at ground level does nothing to restore the ozone layer

e) How could *you* personally help to prevent the destruction of the ozone layer?

17 Copy and complete this table, which shows some of the harmful consequences of human activities and past mistakes, and possible remedies. (The first one has been done for you as an example.)

Human activities	Consequences	Remedies
Burning fossil fuels	respiratory diseases and blackening of buildings	smokeless zones, alternative fuels
	decrease in number of whales	
	destruction of tropical rain forests	
	pollution of river water	
	mutations in sex cells of ovary and testis	
	damage to inner ear	
	photochemical smog	
	reduction in variety of British wildlife	

Theme 3

The Basic Organisation of Living Things

1 Plant and Animal Cells

1 Copy this paragraph and fill in the missing words:

Organisms are made of basic units called _____ . They were first named by
_____ in the _____ century. He observed the cells in a piece of
_____ . He saw them by using a _____ which he had made himself.
This _____ the cells so that he was able to see them clearly.

2 a) Copy this diagram of a **typical animal cell** and label the cell membrane,
      cytoplasm and nucleus:

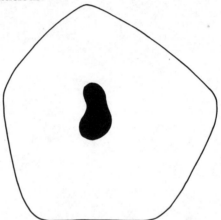

   b) What would be the actual size of such a cell if it came from the lining of your
       cheek?

3 Copy this diagram of a **typical plant cell** and label the following:

cell membrane   cell wall   chloroplast   cytoplasm   nucleus
vacuole

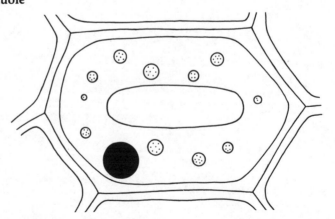

4 Copy the table below. Complete it by putting a tick if the structure in the first column is present and a cross if it is not.

Structure	Typical animal cell (e.g. cheek cell)	Typical plant cell (e.g. moss leaf cell)
Cell membrane		
Cell wall		
Chloroplasts		
Cytoplasm		
Nucleus		
Vacuole		

Did You Know?
A fully grown human is made up of about one hundred million million cells.

5 Match the following **cell structures** with their correct description:

Cell Structure	Description
cell membrane	the granular material in which the nucleus is embedded
cell wall	a large fluid-filled cavity in the middle of a plant cell
chloroplasts	thread-like bodies found inside the nucleus
chromosomes	a thin structure which surrounds the cytoplasm
cytoplasm	structures which release energy
mitochondria	the structure which controls the cytoplasm; without it, the cell almost always dies
nucleus	structures which contain the green pigment chlorophyll
vacuole	the outer boundary of plant cells; made of cellulose

6 Below are five pairs of statements about animal or plant cells. Sort them into two groups:

Animal cells	Plant cells

a) They are surrounded only by a thin cell membrane.
They have a cellulose cell wall in addition to a cell membrane.

b) They have a large central vacuole.
They do not have a large central vacuole.

c) The cytoplasm fills the cell.
    The cytoplasm is pushed towards the edge of the cell.

d) The cytoplasm contains chloroplasts.
    The cytoplasm does not contain chloroplasts.

e) Food is stored as starch.
    Food is stored as glycogen.

> *Did You Know?*
> There are about 200 different types of cell
> in the human body.

7 a) Copy the following diagrams of some **specialised cells**:

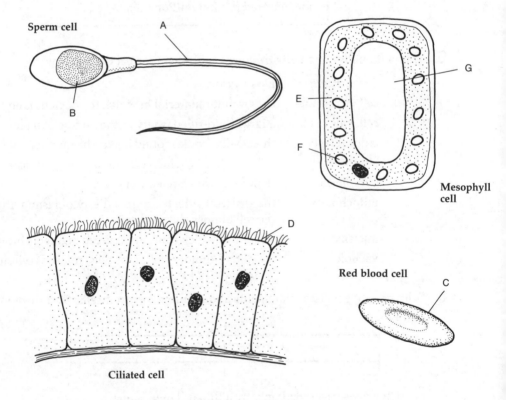

b) Replace the letters A–G with the correct label chosen from the list below.

        vacuole   biconcave disc   cilia   tail   chloroplast
        haploid nucleus   cytoplasm

c) For each feature given in the table below suggest a reason.

Feature	Reason
Sperm cells have a whip-like tail.	
Sperm cells release dissolving enzymes from the tip of the head.	
Sperm cells contain many mitochondria.	
Red blood cells have a large surface area.	
Red blood cells have a thin membrane.	
Red blood cells are packed with molecules of haemoglobin.	
Cilia continually flicker and move.	
Ciliated cells line the trachea and oviducts.	
Mesophyll cells have lots of chloroplasts.	
Mesophyll cells are positioned in the upper part of the leaf.	

2 Looking at Cells

1 This diagram shows the main parts of a typical **light microscope**.

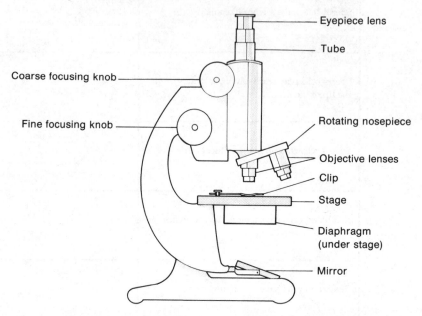

Answer the following questions about how to use this type of microscope.

a) How is a glass slide held in position on the stage?

b) Why must the specimen on the slide be in the centre of the hole in the stage?

c) Why does the nosepiece rotate?

d) What is the mirror for?

e) How can you control the amount of light coming through the microscope?

f) Explain how you would use the microscope to look at a specimen under low power.

g) If you had a specimen in focus under low power, how would you go on to look at it under high power?

h) Why should you never rack downwards with the coarse focusing knob while you are looking down the microscope?

i) If the magnifying power of the eyepiece lens is ten times ($\times 10$), and that of the low power objective lens is four times ($\times 4$), what is the total magnification of a specimen under low power?

j) If the magnifying power of the eyepiece lens is $\times 10$, and that of the high power objective lens is $\times 40$, what is the total magnification of a specimen under high power?

2   The diagrams below show a specimen mounted on a slide ready for viewing under the microscope. Look at them and answer the questions below.

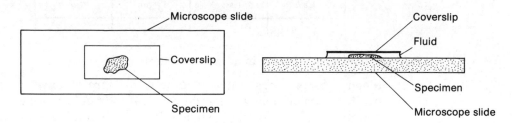

a)   What is the purpose of the coverslip?

b)   This diagram shows how to lower a coverslip on to a specimen.

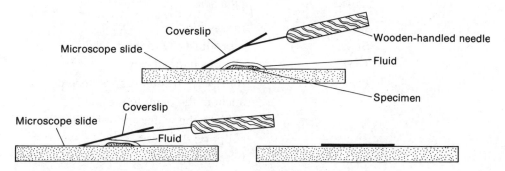

Why is it important to lower the coverslip in this way?

c)   The fluid used may be either pure water or a stain. Give one advantage and one disadvantage of using a stain.

d)   Describe in *words* how to prepare a slide for the microscope. Use the diagrams to help you.

3 Tissues, Organs and Organisms

1   Use words from the following list to complete the sentences below:

        cells   tissues   organ   system   organisms

a)   Large numbers of _____ that have the same structure and function are grouped together to form _____ .

b)   In most _____ , tissues are grouped together to form _____ .

c)   _____ are complex structures with a particular job to do.

d)   Several different organs work together in a _____ .

2 Construct a table with the following headings:

Cell	Tissue	Organ	Organism

Put each word from this list in its correct column in the table:

> blood   brain   egg   eye   epidermis   fern   flower   frog
> heart   human kidney   ladybird   leaf   liver   muscle
> neurone   root   sperm   stem   testes   windpipe   xylem

3 Match the following plant organs with their correct function(s):

Organ	Function
Root	makes food
Stem	reproduces by making seeds
Leaf	absorbs light energy
Flower	transports substances between parts of the plant
	anchors the plant to the soil
	absorbs the water and mineral salts
	supports the plant
	releases and receives pollen

4 Copy and complete the table below about the **major organ systems in a mammal**.

Name of system	Main organs in the system	Main functions
	Gut, liver and pancreas	
		To take in oxygen and get rid of carbon dioxide
		To carry oxygen and food round the body
	Kidneys, bladder, liver	
	Eyes, ears, nose	To detect stimuli
Nervous system		
Musculo-skeletal system		To support and move the body
Reproductive system		

5 a) Copy this diagram of an imaginary organism:

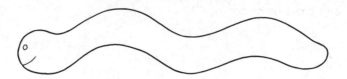

b) Write the following words in the correct position on the diagram:

anterior   dorsal   posterior   ventral

---

4 Movement In and Out of Cells

---

1 Copy and complete this sentence, choosing the correct word given in the brackets:

> Diffusion results in molecules moving from a region of (high/low) concentration to a region where they are (less/more) concentrated.

2 Copy and complete the following sentences by filling in the missing words:

a) **Diffusion** is important because it is the main way in which living organisms obtain the things they _require_, and get rid of their _waste_ products. Here are some examples.

b) Oxygen continually _passes_ into the body of *Amoeba* and _CO_2_ continually diffuses out. This is because *Amoeba* constantly uses _O_2_ and produces _CO_2_.

c) The same process also occurs in our lungs. The _O_2_ diffuses from the lungs into the blood. The _CO_2_ diffuses from the blood into the lungs.

d) In our gut soluble food substances such as glucose _diffuse_ from the intestine into the surrounding blood capillaries.

e) Green leaves obtain the gas _CO_2_ for photosynthesis by diffusion. It enters the leaf through small holes or pores.

f) Fishes obtain _O_2_ from the water by diffusion. As the water flows past the gills, oxygen _diffuses_ from the water into the blood. Carbon dioxide diffuses from the _blood_ into the water.

3 Copy and complete this sentence about **osmosis** by filling in the missing words:

> Osmosis involves the diffusion of _water_ from a _lw_ to a more concentrated solution, separated by a _semi_ permeable membrane.

4 Copy the diagram below of an **osmometer**. Some of the following statements about it are true, and others are false. Decide which are the correct statements and write them down.

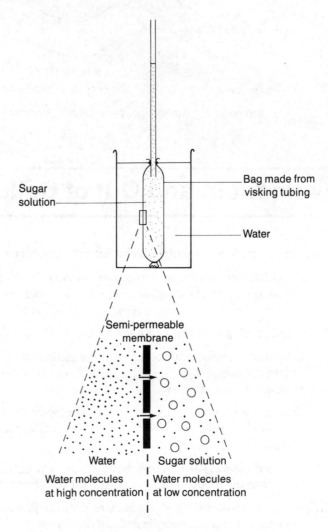

Sugar solution

Bag made from visking tubing

Water

Semi-permeable membrane

Water

Sugar solution

Water molecules at high concentration

Water molecules at low concentration

✗ a)   All the molecules are the same size.

✓ b)   Water molecules are smaller than sugar molecules.

✓ c)   Water molecules can pass in and out of the bag.

✗ d)   Sugar molecules can pass in and out of the bag.

✓ e)   Sugar molecules cannot pass out of the bag.

✗ f)   There are more water molecules inside the bag.

✓ g)   There are more water molecules outside the bag.

✗ h)   Water molecules move from low to high concentration.

✓ i) Water molecules move from high to low concentration.

✓ j) Water molecules move into the bag.

✗ k) Water molecules move out of the bag.

✗ l) Sugar molecules move out of the bag.

✗ m) Sugar molecules move into the bag.

✓ n) The volume of the bag increases.

✗ o) The volume of the bag decreases.

✓ p) The level of the liquid in the tube rises.

✗ q) The level of the liquid in the tube falls.

✗ r) The water level in the beaker rises.

✓ s) The water level in the beaker falls.

5 Suppose a partially permeable bag (as in question 4) was filled with a 20% sugar solution. What would happen to the volume of liquid inside the bag if it was surrounded by the following? Give reasons in each case.

a) distilled water   _increase_

b) 5% sugar solution   _decrese_

c) 20% sugar solution   _nothing_

d) 40% sugar solution   _increse_

6 Copy and complete the following sentences about **animal cells and osmosis**. Choose the best word or words from the three given.

a) Animal cells contain ...

 i) salt.

 ii) a solution of salts and other substances.   ✓

 iii) water.

b) Animal cells are enclosed by ...

 i) a cell wall.

 ii) a permeable membrane.

 iii) a partially permeable membrane.   ✓

c) When placed in water animal cells ...

 i) swell up and burst.   ✓

 ii) shrink and wrinkle.

 iii) remain the same.

d) When animal cells are put into a strong salt solution they ...

   i)   swell up and burst.

   ii)   shrink and wrinkle. ✓

   iii) remain the same.

7 Copy and complete the following sentences about **plant cells and osmosis**. Choose the best answer from the three given.

a) In the centre of a plant cell there is a vacuole which contains ...

   i)   salt.

   ii)   a solution of salts and other substances. ✓

   iii) water.

b) Plant cells are enclosed by ...

   i)   a cell wall.

   ii)   a cell membrane.

   iii) a cell wall and cell membrane. ✓

c) The cell wall is ...

   i)   fully permeable. ✓

   ii)   partially permeable.

   iii) non-permeable.

d) The cell membrane is ...

   i)   fully permeable.

   ii)   partially permeable. ✓

   iii) non-permeable.

e) A plant cell put into water ...

   i)   shrinks and crinkles.

   ii)   swells and becomes turgid or firm. ✓

   iii) remains the same.

f) A plant cell put into a strong salt solution ...

   i)   swells and becomes turgid. ✓

   ii)   remains the same.

   iii) becomes soft and plasmolysed.

8 Below are two simple diagrams of **plant cells in different conditions**. Draw the cells and then answer the questions.

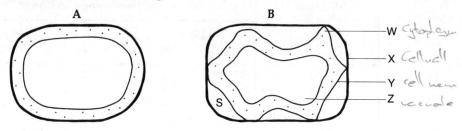

A   B

W Cytoplasm
X Cell wall
Y cell mem
Z vacuole

S

a) Which cell has been placed in distilled water?   A

b) Which cell has been placed in strong sugar solution?   B

c) Which cell is turgid?   A

d) Which cell is plasmolysed?   B

e) In plant cell B

   i)   what do the labels W, X, Y and Z represent?

   ii) what is found in the space marked S?

f) Explain in your own words what has happened to plant cell B.

9 An experiment to demonstrate **active transport in roots** was set up in the following way.

Two similar groups of plants were grown in culture solutions as shown below.

During the experiment oxygen was bubbled through the solutions of Group A and nitrogen was bubbled through the solutions of Group B. The amount of ions taken up by the plants was measured in each case.

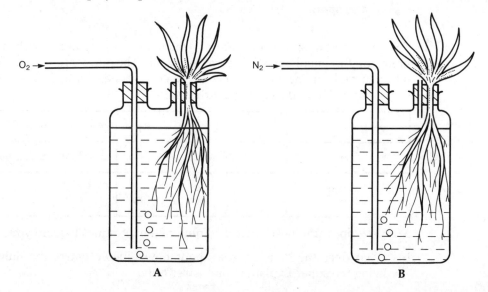

$O_2 \rightarrow$ $N_2 \rightarrow$

A   B

The results for each culture solution are given in the following table:

Time (minutes)	Total amount of mineral ions absorbed (in arbitrary units)	
	Group A with oxygen (aerobic)	Group B with nitrogen (anaerobic)
0	0	0
30	210	130
60	280	180
90	340	200
120	380	215
150	420	228
180	480	240
210	490	250
240	520	280

a) Plot a graph of these results, putting 'Time' on the horizontal axis.

b) In which solution did the plants take up most mineral ions?

c) What process taking place in the roots uses oxygen?

d) Write an equation to summarise this process.

e) Why does giving the roots plenty of oxygen affect the uptake of mineral ions?

f) Why does over-watering pot plants often kill them?

10 Copy and complete these sentences about **active transport**.

Cells take up some substances by _____ them across the cell membrane _____ the concentration gradient. This is an active process and needs _____ from respiration. This is called **active transport**.

11 The table below shows the rate at which two sugars are absorbed into the lining of the small intestine of a mammal. The rates are shown for living intestine and for intestine which has been poisoned with a substance which stops respiration in the cells lining the intestine.

	Rate of absorption (in arbitrary units)	
Sugar	Living intestine	Poisoned intestine
Arabinose	29	29
Glucose	100	33

a) How does arabinose enter the lining of the intestine? Explain your answer.

b) What does the data suggest about how glucose enters the lining of the living intestine? Explain your answer fully.

5 The Chemistry of Life

1 The following are some of the **elements** that occur in organisms. Answer the questions about them.

> calcium   carbon   hydrogen   iron   magnesium   nitrogen
> oxygen   sodium

a) Which *four* elements are found in organisms in the greatest amounts?

b) Name *one* element not given in the list, which is found in organisms such as humans.

c) Which of the elements occur in

   i)   water?

   ii)   carbohydrates?

   iii) fats?

   iv)   proteins?

2 a) Copy and complete this table:

Type of substance	Description	Examples
Inorganic	Simple substances, usually lack carbon	
Organic		Carbohydrates, fats, proteins

b) Name one important inorganic substance that contains carbon.

3 Glucose, starch and sucrose are **carbohydrates**. Answer these questions about them.

a) Which one is a single sugar or monosaccharide?

b) Which one is a double sugar or disaccharide?

c) Which one is a multiple sugar or polysaccharide?

d) Which two are soluble in water?

e) Which one is insoluble in water?

f) Which one is the main substance from which living things obtain energy?

g) What is the chemical formula of glucose?

h) Draw simple diagrams to show the structure of these three carbohydrates.

4 Copy and complete these sentences about **fats**:

a) Fats are made up of smaller units called _____ and _____.

b) Different kinds of fats contain different _____.

c) One function of fat is to give us _____.

d) Many fats provide a source of fat-soluble _____.

5 Copy and complete these sentences about **protein**:

a) Proteins are made up of smaller units called _____.

b) About _____ different amino acids occur in nature.

c) Small chains of amino acids are called _____.

d) Some proteins are tough and fibre-like, forming structures such as hair, _____ and _____.

e) Substances called _____ are proteins that control the rate of chemical reactions in the body.

---

6 Enzymes

---

1 Choose words from this list to complete the following sentences about enzymes.

> catalysts   destroyed   neutral   organisms
> proteins   reactions   specific

a) Enzymes are _____ which speed up the chemical _____ which occur in _____. They are 'biological _____.

b) Enzymes are _____ in that they can only control one type of reaction.

c) Enzymes are _____ by excess heat and are also sensitive to changes in pH. Most enzymes work best in _____ conditions.

2 The following results were obtained from an experiment in which saliva was mixed with a starch suspension. Samples of the mixture were kept in water baths at different temperatures for 15 minutes. At the end of this time the samples were analysed to find out how much sugar had been produced in each. The results are given below.

Temperature (°C)	0	10	20	30	40	50	60	70	80
Units of sugar	12	36	65	90	90	60	30	4	2

a) Plot a line graph of these results, labelling the axes as shown.

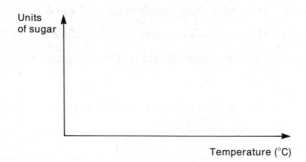

b) What kind of substance must be present in the saliva to break down the starch into sugar?

c) At which temperatures is most sugar produced?

d) Why is very little sugar formed when the saliva and starch mixture are kept at a high temperature?

e) What other factors, besides temperature, would affect the amount of sugar produced from a starch and saliva mixture?

f) Can saliva break down any substances other than starch? Explain your answer.

3 Hydrogen peroxide can be broken down by catalysts into water and oxygen. In an experiment to investigate this reaction, samples of fresh and previously boiled materials were added to samples of hydrogen peroxide in test tubes. Any gas evolved was tested for oxygen. The results are shown below.

Test-tube	Contents	Test on gas evolved
1	Hydrogen peroxide	No oxygen evolved
2	Hydrogen peroxide + fresh manganese dioxide	Oxygen evolved
3	Hydrogen peroxide + boiled manganese dioxide	Oxygen evolved
4	Hydrogen peroxide + fresh liver	Oxygen evolved
5	Hydrogen peroxide + boiled liver	No oxygen evolved
6	Hydrogen peroxide + fresh blood	Oxygen evolved
7	Hydrogen peroxide + boiled blood	No oxygen evolved

a) What would you see happening in the test tubes as gas is evolved?

b) How would you test the gas for oxygen?

c) Why was tube 1 set up?

d) Explain carefully what has happened in tube 2.

e) Explain the results which occur in tubes 4 and 6.

f) Explain why the result obtained in tube 3 differs from that in tubes 5 and 7.

g) State *two* factors which should be kept constant in all seven tubes.

4 a) The table below gives some **uses of enzymes**. Copy and complete it.

Use	Enzyme involved	Explanation
Washing clothes	Proteases	Biological washing powders dissolve protein stains e.g. blood.
Tenderising meat	Proteases	
Making syrup and fruit juice		Starch is broken down into sweet sugars.
	Cellulase	The tough cellulose cell walls are broken down.
Cheese making	Rennin	

b) The biological action of washing powder is reduced if the temperature of the wash is too high. Explain this.

Theme 4

Life Processes

1 Food and Diet

1 Using the following words, write a few sentences to explain why we and all other organisms need food:

       energy   **warmth**   **growth**   **repair**   **healthy**   **movement**

2 A balanced diet consists of roughage (or dietary fibre) plus six other substances; what are they?

3 Complete these sentences about food, choosing the correct word or words from inside the brackets.

    a) Sugar is needed for (roughage/energy) and is found in (meat/cakes).

    b) Fat is needed for (growth and repair/insulation) and is found in (bread/butter).

    c) Protein is needed for (growth and repair/insulation) and is found in (meat/ toffee).

4 Complete the following sentences:

    a) Starch consists of smaller units called _____ .

    b) Protein consists of smaller units called _____ .

    c) Fats consist of smaller units called _____ .

5 Complete this table by placing a tick under each element that is found in the foods given:

	Carbon	Hydrogen	Oxygen	Nitrogen
Carbohydrate				
Protein				
Fat				

6 Complete the following table about food tests:

	Sugar	Starch	Protein	Fat
What are the testing reagents?				
Is heat required?				
What is the colour of a positive test?				

7 A pupil was given five powders A, B, C, D and E. Each powder was tested for the presence of

> **Glucose – using Benedict's test**
> **Starch – using the iodine test**
> **Protein – using the biuret test**

The table of results below shows the final colour observed at the end of each of the tests.

	Powder A	Powder B	Powder C	Powder D	Powder E
Benedict's test	orange	blue	blue	orange	blue
Iodine test	black	black	yellow/brown	black	yellow/brown
Biuret test	blue	blue	purple	purple	blue

Which powder contained

a) protein only?

b) starch only?

c) starch and glucose only?

d) glucose, starch and protein?

e) none of these substances?

8 a) What is roughage (or dietary fibre)?

b) Why is it important in the diet?

c) List *six* foods that are high in fibre.

2 Diet and Good Health

1 From the information below write a complete sentence about each of the following **minerals** we need in our diet:

Mineral	Where found (source)	Function
Sodium	table salt	helps to keep body fluids, e.g. blood, at the right concentration
Calcium	milk and cheese	hardens bones and teeth
Iron	meat and liver	helps to make haemoglobin
Iodine	sea food	helps to make thyroxine
Fluorine	water supply	helps to prevent tooth decay

2 Complete the following table on **vitamins** by filling in the spaces:

Vitamin	Source	Deficiency disease
	carrots	night blindness
B₁ (thiamine)	yeast and cereal	
B (niacin)	meat and fish	
	oranges and lemons	
		rickets

3 In the early 1900s Sir Frederick Gowland Hopkins performed experiments on rats and their diet. In one experiment he divided some rats from the same litter into two groups. Group A were fed on purified cheese protein, glucose, starch, lard, minerals and water. Group B received exactly the same food plus 3 cm³ of milk per day. After 18 days Group A instead of Group B were given the milk. The results are shown below.

Time /days	Average mass of rats in Group A /g	Average mass of rats in Group B /g
0	45	45
5	48	55
10	52	64
15	50	73
20	46	80
25	50	85
30	60	86
35	65	87
40	70	87
45	76	82
50	82	75

Plot the results on a graph, putting 'Time /days' on the horizontal axis. Above day 18 draw a vertical dotted line to show where the diets were changed.

Now study your graph and try to answer these questions:

a) Why did Gowland Hopkins use two groups of rats rather than two individuals?

b) Why did he use rats that all came from the same litter?

c) What was the average mass of rats in Groups A and B on day 18?

d) On which days were the masses of Groups A and B equal?

e) After the change of diet on day 18 what happened to Group B's mass and why?

f) After the change of diet on day 18 why did the mass of Group A not rise immediately?

g) Why did Gowland Hopkins change the diets over?

h) Other than milk, why was it important that both Groups of rats should receive equal amounts of food and water?

i) If the experiment had been continued for a further 20 days what do you think would have happened to the masses of Groups A and B?

j) What conclusions did Gowland Hopkins come to after seeing the results of this experiment?

4 What are the benefits to health of the following dietary recommendations?

a) To consume the quantity of food and drink which will help you maintain a body weight which is ideal for your height.

b) To reduce fat intake, especially saturated animal fat.

c) To eat less sugar (sucrose).

d) To increase dietary fibre to an average of between 25 and 30 grams per day.

e) To eat less salt.

f) To reduce alcohol consumption to a moderate amount.

Did You Know?
The use of food additives is so widespread that the average person probably consumes about five kilograms in a year.

---

5 a) What is meant by a food additive?

b) List *five* reasons why additives are used by the food industry.

c) What is an 'E number'?

d) How can you find out which chemicals have been added to the food you buy?

e) In many food products, artificial colourings such as tartrazine (E102) are being replaced by natural colourings. Why is this beneficial to the health of many people?

6 a) What is malnutrition?

   b) What are the causes and symptoms of the following nutritional disorders?
       i)   obesity
       ii)   kwashiorkor
       iii) marasmus
       iv)   anorexia nervosa
       v)   anaemia
       vi)   goitre

   c) Why did Admiral Nelson insist that British ships should carry an ample supply of limes?

3 Teeth

1 Complete the following table about **human teeth**:

Name of tooth	Diagram of shape of tooth	Total number in milk set	Total number in permanent set	Main function
Incisor				
Canine				
Premolar				
Molar				

2 Make a large copy of the following diagram, which shows the **internal structure of a tooth**:

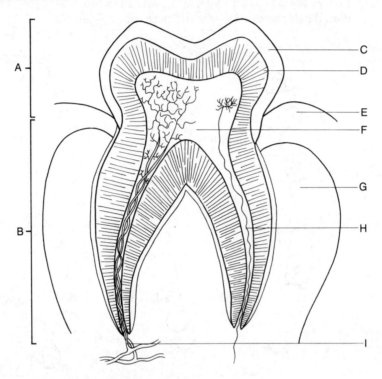

a) What is the name of this type of tooth?

b) Replace the letters A to I with the correct labels chosen from the list below:

blood capillaries   crown   dentine   enamel   gum
jawbone   nerves   pulp cavity   root

c) Study the above diagram and complete the following sentences by filling in the missing word or words:

i) The part of the tooth which can be seen is called the _____ .

ii) The _____ is embedded in the gum.

iii) _____ is the hardest substance in the body.

iv) _____ forms the bulk of the tooth and decays easily.

v) The _____ contains the nerve and blood supply to the tooth.

d) Why do you think blood capillaries are present in the centre of the tooth?

3 Write a short account of **tooth decay** and its prevention including the following words:

bacteria   plaque   sugary food   acid   enamel   proper diet
thorough brushing   fluoride toothpaste   dentist

4 The diagrams below show plans of teeth in the upper and lower jaw.

Plan A belongs to a 25-year-old man called Mike.
Plan B belongs to a 25-year-old man called Peter.

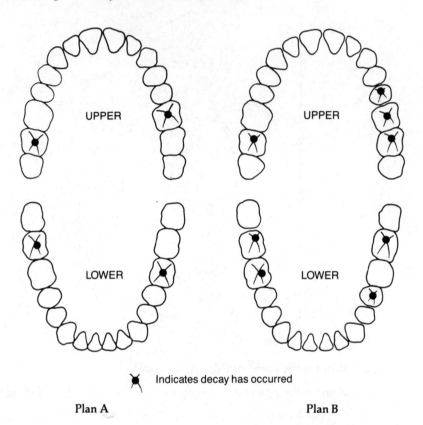

✖ Indicates decay has occurred

Plan A   Plan B

In the town where Mike lives the drinking water contains natural fluoride salts. There are no fluoride salts in the drinking water where Peter lives.

a) How many decayed teeth has

   i) Mike?

   ii) Peter?

b) What is the percentage of decayed teeth in

   i) Mike?

   ii) Peter?

c) Suggest *five* possible reasons why Peter has more decayed teeth than Mike.

d) Explain why it is the back teeth that have mostly decayed.

e) Give *two* reasons why the sets of teeth shown in the diagram must be permanent teeth rather than milk teeth.

4 Feeding in Mammals

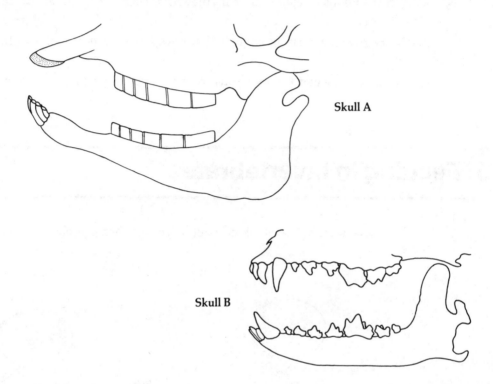

Skull A

Skull B

1 Study the diagrams above of the two skulls A and B, and then complete the following table by using the words 'yes' or 'no':

	Skull A	Skull B
Does the animal eat plant matter (herbivore)?		
Does the animal eat other animals (carnivore)?		
Is there a gap between the front and back teeth for holding food?		
Are the upper incisors replaced by a hard pad?		
Are the canines missing or reduced in size?		
Are the canines large and dagger-like?		
Are the cheek teeth jagged?		
Do the cheek teeth have a flat grinding surface?		

2 Now copy the diagram of skull A and underneath it write a few sentences describing how this animal uses its teeth and jaws to feed. Then do the same for skull B.

3 a) Name *four* plant-eating animals that have cheek teeth similar to those in skull A.

   b) Name *four* meat-eating animals that have large canines similar to those in skull B.

   c) What does the word 'omnivorous' mean? Name *two* omnivorous animals.

5 Feeding in Invertebrates

1 Study the diagrams below of insect mouthparts and then complete the following table.

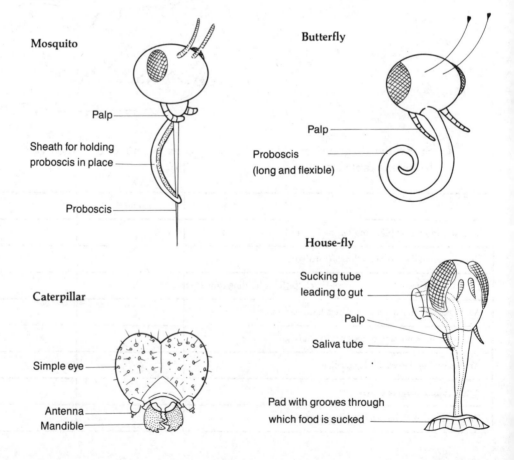

Mosquito

Palp

Sheath for holding
proboscis in place

Proboscis

Butterfly

Palp

Proboscis
(long and flexible)

House-fly

Sucking tube
leading to gut

Palp

Saliva tube

Pad with grooves through
which food is sucked

Caterpillar

Simple eye

Antenna
Mandible

Name of insect	Example of food on which the insect feeds	In what way are the insect's mouthparts specialised for feeding?

2 Using a library, try to find out how these invertebrates feed:

> sea anemone   barnacle   limpet   scorpion   fan worm
> crab   cockle   starfish

3 Below is a vivid description of a man being attacked by an animal. Can you identify the animal?

> I could have sworn the brute's eyes burned at me as I turned in towards his cranny. I remember a dreadful sliminess. Something whipped round my left arm and the back of my neck, binding the two together. In the same flash, another something slapped itself high on my forehead, and I felt it crawling down inside the back of my vest. A mouth began to nuzzle below my throat, at the junction of the collar-bones. The cables around me tightened painfully. My mouth was smothered by some flabby moving horror. The suckers felt like hot rings pulling at my skin.
>
> Abridged and adapted from *A Pattern of Islands* by Arthur Grimble

6 Digesting Food

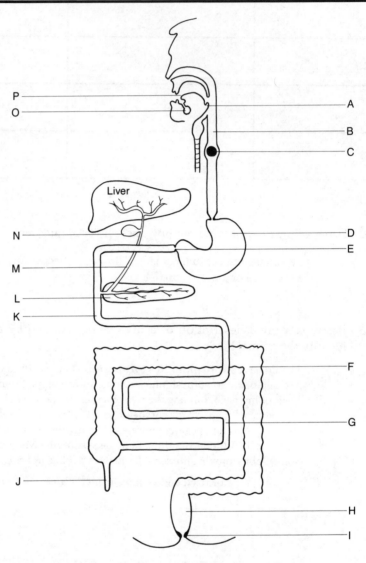

1 Copy the above diagram, which represents the human gut. Replace the letters A–P with the correct labels chosen from the list provided:

anus   appendix   bile duct   bolus of food   colon   duodenum
epiglottis   gall bladder   ileum   mouth   oesphagus   pancreas
pyloric sphincter muscle   rectum   salivary gland   stomach

> *Did You Know?*
> The human gut is approximately 8 metres long.

2 From the two lists below match each structure with its correct function. (The first one has been done for you as an example.)

Salivary glands ... produce saliva

Structure	*Function*
Salivary glands	produces enzymes which pass into the duodenum
The oesophagus	controls the passing of faeces
The stomach	produce saliva
The pyloric sphincter muscle	is where most water is absorbed
The duodenum	carries food from the mouth to the stomach
The ileum	stores bile
The bile duct	receives juices from the gall bladder and pancreas
The pancreas	controls the amount of food leaving the stomach
The gall bladder	stores waste faeces for several hours
The colon	produces hydrochloric acid
The rectum	is where most digested food is absorbed
The anus	takes bile from the gall bladder to the duodenum

3 Complete these sentences about **what happens in the gut**, by filling in the missing words:

An egg sandwich contains starch, fat and protein: the starch is in the _____, most of the fat is in the _____ and much of the protein is in the _____. When this sandwich enters your _____ it is chopped up into small pieces by your teeth. This increases the _____ of the food so that the digestive enzymes of the gut can act more quickly. These enzymes break the food down even more, changing _____ molecules like starch into _____ soluble molecules such as glucose. These soluble molecules can pass through the lining of the gut into the _____.

4 Answer the following questions about **the way we digest our food**:

a) Saliva contains water together with two other important substances. What are they?

b) What are the main functions of saliva?

c) How is solid food moved down the gullet (oesophagus)?

d) What is this process called?

e) What structure prevents food from entering the windpipe?

f) Name one digestive enzyme produced by the stomach wall, and the type of food substance it helps to break up?

g) The stomach also produces acid. What is this acid for?

h) How is the stomach wall protected from the acid?

i) How does the muscle in the wall of the stomach help digestion?

j) The digestive enzymes of the small intestine work best in alkaline conditions; how, therefore, is the acid from the stomach neutralised?

k) Where is bile

    i) made?

    ii) stored?

    iii) mixed with food?

l) What does bile do?

m) The pancreas produces a juice which contains three important enzymes; name the enzyme which acts upon

    i) starch

    ii) protein

    iii) fat

n) Why must food be digested before it can be absorbed?

o) Give *two* ways in which the wall of the small intestine is adapted to absorb digested food.

p) As a result of digestion what are the following foods finally broken down into:

    i) starch

    ii) protein

    iii) fat

q) Why is roughage (or dietary fibre) important in the human diet?

Did You Know?
The record for constipation is 102 days.

5 Complete the following table to show where starch, protein and fat are digested in the human gut. Put ticks in the correct boxes. (The first one has been done for you as an example.)

	Starch	Protein	Fat
Mouth	✓	—	—
Oesophagus			
Stomach			
Small intestine			
Large intestine			

6 Complete the following table by filling in the blank spaces:

Enzymes	Where produced	Where mixed with food	Food acted on (substrate)	Substances produced (products)
		mouth		maltose
Pepsin				polypeptides
	pancreas		starch	
Lipase				
			proteins and polypeptides	
Maltase				
Peptidases			peptides	

7 a) Study the details of the experiment described below, and then complete the table by filling in the results that would be expected in each test-tube.

Three mixtures contained in test-tubes were set up as follows:
Tube A: 1% starch solution plus amylase at 37 °C
Tube B: 1% starch solution plus boiled amylase at 37 °C
Tube C: 1% starch solution plus acid plus amylase at 37 °C
After twenty minutes samples from each tube were tested with iodine solution and Benedict's or Fehling's reagent.

	Colour of Tube A	Colour of Tube B	Colour of Tube C
Tested with iodine solution			
Tested with Benedict's or Fehling's reagent			

b) Where would you find amylase being secreted in the human digestive system?

c) Why are the tubes kept at 37 °C?

d) Where are the conditions found in Tube C likely to occur in the human digestive system?

> *Did You Know?*
> Every day we secrete about 1 litre of saliva.

8 The table below shows the time taken for the complete breakdown of a sample of starch suspension in the presence of an enzyme in solutions of different pH.

Time taken (minutes)	6	4.5	3	2	1.25	1.25	3
pH	5	5.5	6	6.5	7	7.5	8

a) Plot these results on graph paper, labelling the axes as shown:

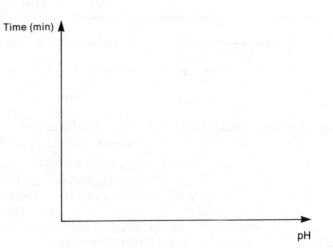

b) At what pH is there the fastest breakdown of the starch solution?

c) Name one region of the gut where this enzyme would *not* work very quickly?

d) How would you prevent a change in temperature from affecting the results of this experiment?

9 The detailed structure of the wall of the small intestine reveals many features that make it well suited to the digestion and absorption of food.

From the diagram below, list as many of these features as you can, under these two headings:

Digestion	*Absorption*

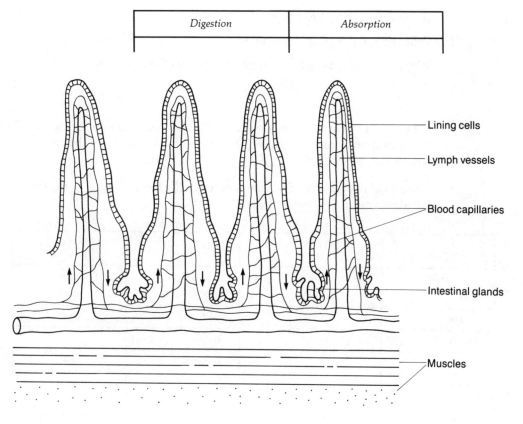

7 Energy from Food

1 a) Which of these substances provide the body with energy?

   carbohydrate   water   fat   mineral salts   protein   vitamins

b) List *five* foods that provide lots of energy.

c)   List *five* foods that provide very little energy.

d)   What units are used to measure the energy value of food?

e)   Describe a simple experiment to show how much energy there is in a small piece of food such as a peanut.

f)   Why does a coal-miner require more energy foods in his diet than a typist?

g)   Name one other occupation with a high daily energy need.

h)   Why does a woman's daily energy need increase when she is

   i)   pregnant?

   ii) breast-feeding her baby?

i)   What happens if people consume more than their daily energy need?

j)   What happens if people consume less than their daily energy need?

2 a)   A healthy 15-year-old needs about 12 000 kilojoules a day. Using the tables below and on the next page, work out a well-balanced diet that meets these requirements.

b)   Make a list of all the food you have eaten in the last 24 hours. Using the tables calculate your daily energy intake.

Food	Energy value (kJ per portion)
Fruit	
Dates	2140
Prunes	840
Banana	460
Pineapple	440
Cherries	390
Apple	380
Grapes	380
Pear	380
Grapefruit	300
Orange	300
Blackcurrants	250
Strawberries	240
Peach	170
Melon	120

Food	Energy value (kJ per portion)
Meat	
Steak	2300
Lamb chop	1800
Beefburgers	1700
Sausages	1600
Roast lamb	1320
Bacon	1300
Roast beef	1100
Boiled ham	1000
Roast chicken	950
Luncheon meat	900
Liver	500
Kidney	300

Food	Energy value (kJ per portion)
Vegetables	
Boiled rice	2600
Chips	1180
Boiled potatoes	500
Baked beans	500
Sweetcorn	350
Peas	230
Brussels sprouts	180
Tomatoes	120
Cabbage	80
Carrots	80
Cauliflower	80
Celery	80
Onions	80
Spinach	80
Lettuce	40
Runner beans	40
Fish	
Fried cod	800
Kipper	800
Sardines	800
Grilled cod	680
Tinned salmon	500
Cereals	
Porridge	630
Cornflakes	380
Puffed wheat	200

Food	Energy value (kJ per portion)
Dairy Produce	
Milk (250 ml)	500
Cheddar cheese	460
Butter	420
Margarine	420
Boiled eggs	380
Whipped cream	210
Cottage cheese	100
Preserves	
Honey	680
Syrup	670
Jam	640
Marmalade	640
Sweets	
Chocolate (60 g)	1380
Toffee (60 g)	1060
Boiled sweets (60 g)	950
Other foods	
Peanuts (50 g)	1320
Spaghetti	690
Cakes	500
Ice-cream	460
Biscuits	450
Bread (slice)	270
Sugar (teaspoon)	100
Drinks	
Squash	450
Lemonade	420
Coffee with milk	110
Tea with milk	70

Did You Know?
During an average lifetime a person eats 20–30 tonnes of food.

3 Copy and complete the following sentence about **how energy is released**. Choose the correct word or words from inside the brackets.

When a piece of food is burned, the gas (oxygen/carbon dioxide) is used up and (carbon dioxide/oxygen) is given off. Water is formed and heat energy is produced.

Now complete the following equation:

Food + ... $\longrightarrow$ .... + water + energy

4 Many experiments can be done to find out if organisms give out carbon dioxide. Here is one of them:

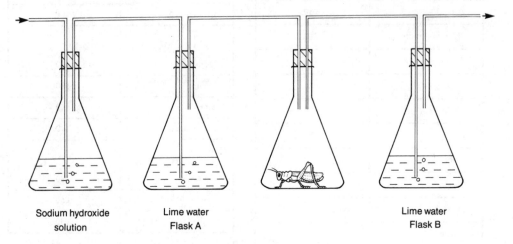

Sodium hydroxide
solution

Lime water
Flask A

Lime water
Flask B

Study the diagram carefully and answer these questions:

a) What does the sodium hydroxide do?

b) What does the limewater in flask A show?

c) What change would you expect to take place in the limewater in flask B after 1 hour?

d) What control would you use in this investigation?

e) Why is it important to use a control?

5 Make a list of as many things as you can think of for which organisms use energy.

6 Which of the following descriptions are true of **respiration**?

a) occurs only in plant cells

b) occurs in all cells

c) takes place only at night

d) produces carbon dioxide

e) uses up energy

f) is affected by temperature

g) takes place all the time

h) produces food

i) produces oxygen

j) uses oxygen

k) uses carbon dioxide

l) produces water

m) releases energy

n) uses water

o) is controlled by enzymes

7 The experiment illustrated below was carried out to find out if living organisms give out heat energy.

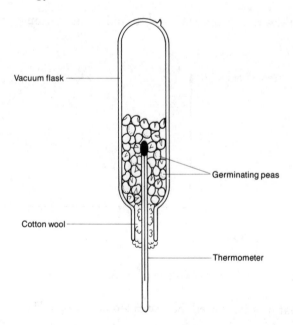

Some pea seeds were divided into three samples of equal mass and then treated as follows:

Sample 1 was soaked in water at 18 °C for 24 hours, and then placed in a sterilised vacuum flask A.

Sample 2 was soaked in water at 18 °C for 24 hours, boiled, cooled to 18 °C and then placed in a sterilised vacuum flask B.

Sample 3 was soaked in water at 18 °C for 24 hours, washed with a very mild disinfectant, and then placed in a sterilised vacuum flask C.

The temperatures inside the three flasks were recorded for 3 days. They are shown below.

	Flask A	*Flask B*	*Flask C*
Start of experiment	18 °C	18 °C	18 °C
After 12 hours	26 °C	18 °C	20 °C
After 24 hours	40 °C	18 °C	23 °C
After 36 hours	48 °C	18 °C	26 °C
After 48 hours	50 °C	18 °C	29 °C
After 60 hours	52 °C	18 °C	33 °C
After 72 hours	54 °C	18 °C	40 °C

a) Plot the results for Flasks A, B and C on the same graph. Label the axes as shown.

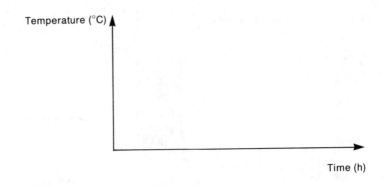

Temperature (°C)

Time (h)

b) Why were vacuum-flasks used instead of ordinary glass flasks?

c) What process caused the rise in temperature in Flasks A and C?

d) Why were the peas soaked before being placed in the flasks?

e) Why was there no temperature rise in Flask B?

f) Why was the temperature rise greater in Flask A than Flask C?

g) Why was Flask B included in the experiment?

8 The apparatus shown below is used to measure **the rate of respiration** in germinating seeds.

   a) What is the purpose of the concentrated potassium hydroxide solution?

   b) What will happen to the coloured liquid in the capillary tubing as the seeds respire? Explain why this happens.

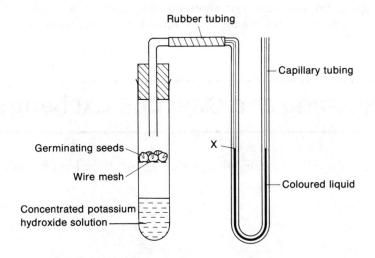

   c) What control should be set up for this experiment?

   d) Name two environmental factors that might affect the level of the liquid at X.

   e) Why is it better to use narrow rather than broad bore capillary tubing?

9 When a peanut is burnt under a test-tube of water, as shown in the diagram, the water heats up.

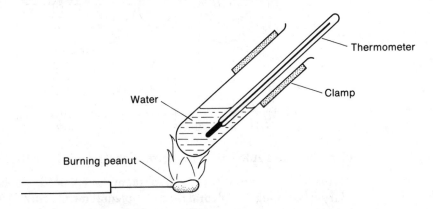

   a) What property of the peanut is being measured?

   b) What measurements must be taken before the peanut is set alight?

c) State *two* safety precautions which must be taken when carrying out the experiment.

d) What measurement must be taken after the peanut has finished burning?

e) State *two* ways in which the result of the experiment may be inaccurate.

f) What piece of apparatus could be used to produce a more accurate result?

g) Using the apparatus shown in the diagram how could you compare the energy values of a peanut, a walnut and a Brazil nut?

8 Breathing and Gaseous Exchange

1 a) Copy the diagram below, which represents the human respiratory system.

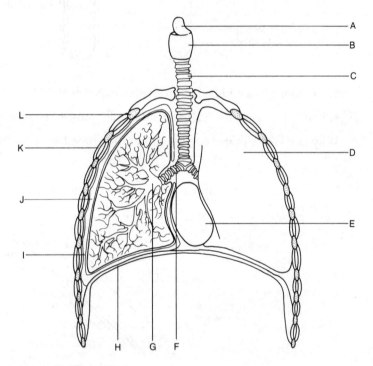

b) Replace the letters A to L with the correct label chosen from the list below:

   bronchiole   bronchus   diaphragm   epiglottis   heart
   larynx   lung   pleural fluid   pleural membranes   ribs
   rib muscle   trachea

c) The diagram shows a vertical section through the human thorax. Why is the left lung smaller than the right?

2 From the two lists below, match each structure with its correct function. (The first
one has been done for you as an example.)

The nasal cavity . . . warms, moistens and filters the air we breathe

Structure	*Function*
a) **The nasal cavity**	protect the lungs and heart
b) **The epiglottis**	separates the thorax from the abdomen
c) **The larynx**	move the rib cage during breathing
d) **The trachea**	that gas exchange takes place
e) **The cartilage rings**	produces sounds
f) **The ribs**	carries air down to the lungs
g) **The intercostal (or rib) muscles**	help to keep the trachea and bronchi open
h) **The pleural fluid**	prevents food from entering the trachea
i) **The diaphragm**	warms, moistens and filters the air we breathe
j) **It is in the alveoli**	prevents friction between the lungs and ribs when breathing

3 Below are eight pairs of statements about **breathing**. Sort them into two groups:

When we breathe in	*When we breathe out*

a) Intercostal muscles contract/Intercostal muscles relax.

b) The rib cage moves up and out/The rib cage moves down and in.

c) The diaphragm muscle relaxes/The diaphragm muscle contracts.

d) The diaphragm moves up/The diaphragm moves down.

e) The diaphragm becomes flatter/The diaphragm becomes dome-shaped.

f) The volume of thorax decreases/The volume of thorax increases.

g) The pressure inside the thorax decreases/The pressure inside the thorax increases.

h) Air is drawn into the lungs/Air is expelled from the lungs.

> *Did You Know?*
> You breathe about 20 000 litres of air every day.

4

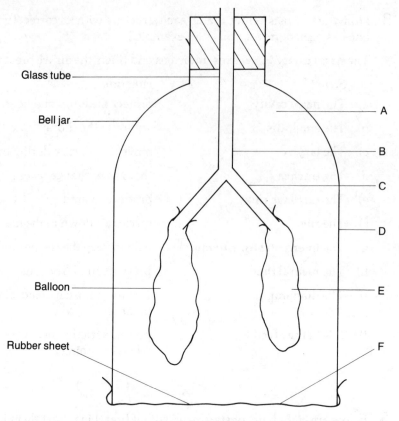

Glass tube

Bell jar

A

B

C

D

Balloon

E

Rubber sheet

F

The diagram above represents a model of the human thorax.

a) What parts of the human thorax do the labels A to F represent?

b) What happens to the balloons when the rubber sheet is pushed upwards? What part of breathing does this represent?

c) What happens to the balloons when the rubber sheet is pulled downwards? What part of breathing does this represent?

d) In what way is this an inaccurate demonstration of how we breathe in and out?

5 Study the table below and then answer the questions.

	Air breathed in (inhaled air)	Air breathed out (exhaled air)
Nitrogen	79.0%	79.0%
Oxygen	20.97%	16.9%
Carbon dioxide	0.03%	4.1%
Water vapour	variable	saturated

a) What happens to the nitrogen we breathe in?

b) Which air sample contains the more oxygen? Explain why.

c) Which air sample contains the more carbon dioxide? Explain why.

d) What does 'saturated' mean?

e) Why does the amount of water vapour in the air vary?

6 Listed below are some features of the alveolar or respiratory surface of the lungs. Say why each feature makes the lung well suited to gas exchange.

Feature	Why it is well suited to gas exchange
Thin	
Moist	
Large surface area	
Rich blood supply	

Did You Know?
There are about 300–750 million alveoli in your lungs.

7 Complete the following passage about **gas exchange** in the lungs by filling in the missing words:

Blood arrives at the lungs in the _____ arteries. This blood is deoxygenated. Oxygen has been used up by the cells of the body during the process of _____ . This blood also contains a lot of _____ . Each pulmonary artery branches many times to form very small vessels called _____ . These are in direct contact with the tiny _____ of the lungs. It is here that _____ exchange takes place. _____ diffuses out of the blood. _____ diffuses into the blood. Oxygenated blood then leaves the lungs in the _____ vein.

8 a) Make a large copy of the following diagram which shows **how gas exchange occurs**:

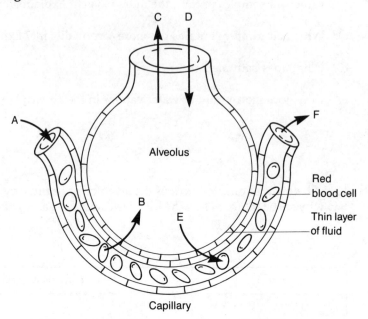

b) Explain what is happening at each of the stages labelled A–F.

9 The diagram below shows microscopic sections of (A) healthy and (B) diseased lung tissue from adult humans.

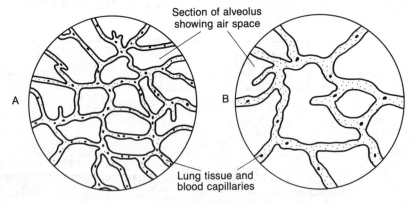

a) What assumption must be made in order to compare the two sections?

b) Give two structural differences between the healthy and the diseased lung which can be seen on the diagrams.

c) Suggest for each difference you have described why it would make the diseased lung work less well.

d) Give two possible causes of the lung damage.

10 a) Copy and complete this table about the **constituents of cigarette smoke**.

Constituent	Effect on the body
	Is addictive. It affects the nervous system, heart and blood vessels
Tar	
	Anaesthetises cilia. It can combine with haemoglobin and reduce the ability of the blood to carry oxygen.

b) Explain how the lungs of smokers tend to become clogged up with mucus.

11 Study the two graphs below, which show **the effects of smoking on health**.

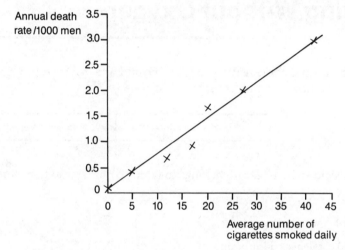

A   Death rate from lung cancer among men smoking different numbers of cigarettes each day

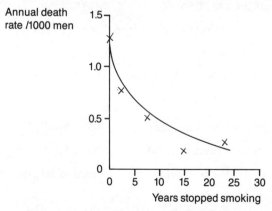

B   Death rate from lung cancer among men who gave up smoking cigarettes

a) Out of a group of 5000 men smoking 30 cigarettes a day, how many are likely to die of lung cancer in one year?

b) What effect does giving up smoking have on a man's chance of contracting lung cancer?

c) Name two harmful substances found in tobacco smoke.

d) Name two diseases other than lung cancer that can be caused by smoking.

e) Why are pregnant women advised not to smoke?

> *Did You Know?*
> A sneeze can travel as fast as 160 km/h – the speed of a hurricane!

9 Living Without Oxygen

1 Below are some features of aerobic and anaerobic respiration. Construct a table with these two headings:

Aerobic respiration	Anaerobic respiration

Decide which feature belongs to which column, and then complete the table.

a) does not need oxygen

b) needs oxygen

c) releases a lot of energy

d) releases a little energy

e) produces ethanol and carbon dioxide in plants

f) produces lactic acid in animals

g) produces carbon dioxide and water in animals and plants

2 a) When do our muscles respire anaerobically?

b) Why can this not go on indefinitely?

c) Why do the following animals need to respire anaerobically for long periods of time?

i) tapeworms

ii) seals

iii) mud-burrowing worms

3 A test-tube containing some yeast and sugar solution was placed in a water bath as shown in the diagram. After ten minutes the rate of bubbling was measured. The experiment was then repeated with the temperature of the water bath at each of the temperatures shown in the table below.

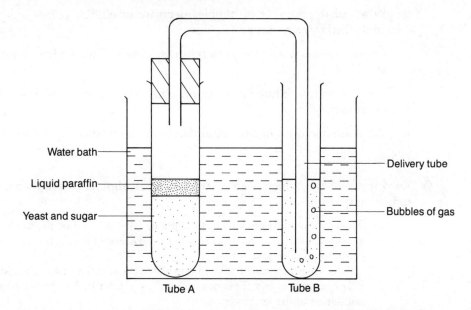

Temperature (°C)	10	20	30	40	50	60
Number of gas bubbles per minute	5	12	20	26	28	14

a) Plot a graph of the results, labelling the axes as shown.

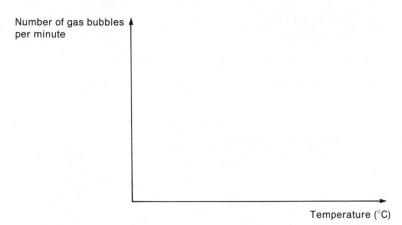

b) What is the function of the liquid paraffin?

c) Give one reason why the apparatus was left for ten minutes at each temperature before any bubbles were counted?

d) Name the process taking place in the yeast cells, which produces the gas.

e) Name the gas being produced.

f) What substance could be used to identify this gas in Tube B?

g) Why did the number of bubbles decrease at 60 °C? (*Clue:* this process is controlled by enzymes.)

h) Give *two* reasons why the yeast cells would die in Tube A after about a week at 40 °C.

i) Write a simple equation to summarise what is happening in the above experiment.

j) What are *two* ways in which humans have taken advantage of this process?

4 Read this passage, which is about **the use of alcohol as a fuel**, then answer the following questions.

> Sugar cane is a fast-growing tropical plant. The sugar it provides can be fermented to make alcohol. Alcohol can be used instead of petrol in cars. It is often mixed with petrol to produce **gasohol**.
>
> After the sugar cane has been crushed to remove the sugar, a woody material called **bagasse** is left. This can be used as a solid fuel to provide heat for the distillation of the fermented sugar.
>
> In Brazil many cars now run on alcohol fuel made this way and Brazil has plans to replace all petrol by alcohol.

a) By what process is the sun's energy converted into chemical energy in the sugar?

b) Explain the meaning of the words 'fermented' and 'distillation'.

c) What is
    i)   gasohol?
    ii) bagasse?

d) Why is it particularly advantageous for Brazil to produce fuel in this way?

e) How is this process an example of biotechnology?

f) To grow enough sugar cane to replace all liquid fuels with alcohol, Brazil would have to create new farmland by clearing parts of the Amazon jungle. What problems would this cause?

10 Blood

1 Copy and complete the following diagram which summarises the **structure of blood**.

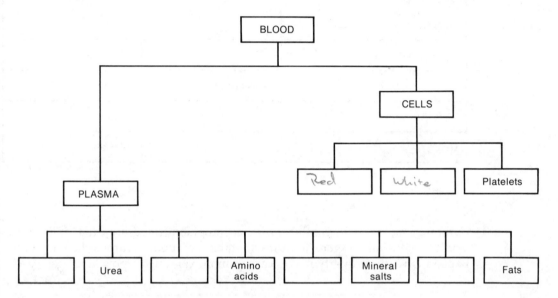

2 Copy and complete the passage below which is about the **structure and function of blood cells**. Choose words from the following list to fill in the blanks. (Some words are used more than once.)

> antibodies   bacteria   biconcave✓   carbon dioxide   clotting
> haemoglobin✓   infection   nucleus✓   oxygen✓   bone marrow✓
> oxyhaemoglobin ✓   platelets   red✓   shape   tissues
> variable   white✓

Blood cells are made in the ~~bone marrow~~. ~~Red~~ blood cells are smaller than ~~white~~ blood cells and there are more of them. Red blood cells are ~~biconcave~~ discs in shape. They have no ~~nucleus~~ and are packed with a substance called ~~haemoglobin~~. In the lungs, ~~oxygen~~ diffuses into red blood cells and combines with ~~haemoglobin~~ to form ~~oxyhaemoglobin~~. In this way oxygen is carried round the body to the ~~tissues~~. Here ~~oxygen~~ is released and oxyhaemoglobin turns back into ~~haemo~~. Red blood cells also carry small amounts of ~~CO₂~~. White blood cells are ~~variable~~ in shape and always contain a ~~nucleus~~. They help the body to fight ~~bacteria~~. Some produce ~~antibodies~~ while others can change ~~shape~~ to engulf ~~bacteria~~ which they then destroy. ~~platelets~~ are tiny fragments of cells which are involved in the ~~clotting~~ of the blood.

3 Copy and complete the following table:

Substance transported in the plasma	From	To
Oxygen (as oxyhaemoglobin)		
Carbon dioxide (as hydrogencarbonate ions)		
Digested food materials		All parts of the body
	Endocrine glands	
	Liver	Kidneys
Heat		All parts of the body

4 Carbon monoxide will combine with haemoglobin three hundred times more readily than will oxygen. It forms a stable compound carboxyhaemoglobin. Explain why this property makes carbon monoxide such a poisonous gas.

> *Did you know?*
> About 120 million red blood cells are produced every minute in the bone marrow!

11 The Heart and Circulation

1 Here is a simple way to draw a **ventral view of the heart**:

   a) Take a full clear page and in the middle draw *very lightly* in pencil, a box 12 cm high and 8 cm wide. Then divide the box into four, so that the top two boxes now measure 4 cm × 4 cm each, and the bottom two 8 cm × 4 cm each.

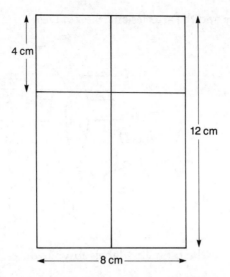

b) Sketch in lightly the shape of the heart and valve as shown below. (This is a ventral view, so the right side of the heart is on the left, and the left side is on the right.)

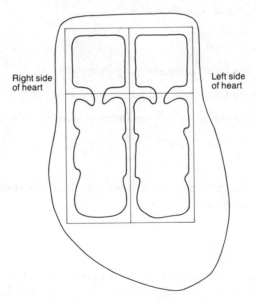

c) Carefully remove the box lines with a rubber.

d) Add the veins – like this:

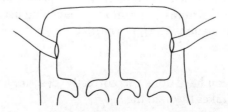

e) Finally add the arteries and their valves:

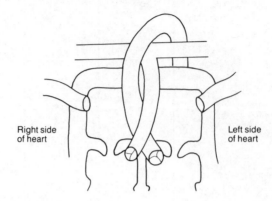

Right side
of heart

Left side
of heart

f) Now add the following labels to your diagram. Remember this is a *ventral* view.

   **right atrium   left atrium   right ventricle   left ventricle
   vena cava   pulmonary artery   aorta   pulmonary vein
   right atrioventricular valve   left atrioventricular valve
   arterial (semi-lunar) valves**

g) Now colour

   i)   the heart muscle lightly in brown

   ii)   the vena cava and pulmonary artery lightly in blue (explaining why)

   iii) the pulmonary vein and dorsal aorta lightly in red (explaining why)

2 On your diagram put small arrows to show the route the blood takes as it flows through the heart.

3 a) Put the following words in the correct sequence to show the order in which the blood flows through the heart. Start with the blood arriving at the heart from the body in the vena cava.

   **left ventricle   vena cava   opening between left atrium and ventricle
   right atrium   aorta   opening between right atrium and ventricle
   left atrium   right ventricle   pulmonary vein   pulmonary artery
   lungs**

   b) Once you have done this correctly, describe in a few sentences the route that blood takes through the heart.

4 Answer the following questions about the heart:

   a) What type of tissue is the heart made of? muscle

   b) What structures inside the heart keep the blood flowing in the right direction?

   c) What is the function of the heart strings?

   d) Explain why the walls of the ventricles are much thicker than those of the atria.

   e) Which chamber of the heart has the thickest wall and why? R. V

   f) Why is the blood that passes through the right side of the heart deoxygenated?

   g) Which chamber pumps blood to the lungs? R. V

   h) Which chamber is the first to receive oxygenated blood from the lungs? R. A

   i) Explain why the wall of the aorta is thicker than the wall of the pulmonary artery.

   j) List *three* ways in which blood in the pulmonary artery differs from blood in the pulmonary vein.

   k) There are many blood vessels running over the surface of the heart; what is their function?

   l) Some babies are born with a 'hole in the heart', which means that there is a hole between the left and right atria. What problems does this cause?

5 If approximately 2000 litres of blood are pumped through the heart each day, what is the total volume pumped

   a) in a week?

   b) in a month (30 days)?

   c) in a year (365 days)?

   d) in 70 years?

6 If the average **heart rate** is 70 beats per minute how many times does the heart beat

   a) in an hour? 4200

   b) in a day? 100 800

   c) in a week? 705 600

   d) in a year? 39513600

   e) in 70 years? 2765952000 !

7 Someone's heart rate was recorded at five-minute intervals. The results are given below.

Time (minutes)	0	5	10	15	20	25	30	35	40	45	50	55	60	65	70	75	80	85	90	95	100	105
Heart beat (beats per minute)	60	60	60	65	68	71	72	72	86	98	105	107	108	105	100	95	88	80	95	74	73	73

a) Plot a graph of these results. Label the axes as shown.

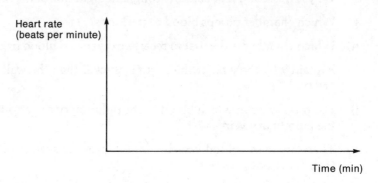

b) From the graph suggest the period of time when this person was

   i)   frightened by a loud bang   90

   ii)   sleeping   0-10mins

   iii) running   40-55

   iv)   waking   15-20.

c) Why does the heart rate need to increase when we are frightened?

8 Copy these sentences about the **effects of exercise** on the body by choosing the correct word from inside the brackets.

a) The depth of breathing goes (up/down).

b) The rate of breathing (decreases/increases).

c) The rate of heart beat goes (up/down).

d) The stroke volume of the heart (rises/falls).

e) (Less/More) oxygen and glucose are supplied to muscle cells.

f) The rate of carbon dioxide removal (increases/decreases).

9 The heart rate of an athlete was recorded before, during and after a race for a total time of 100 minutes. The results are shown in the graph below.

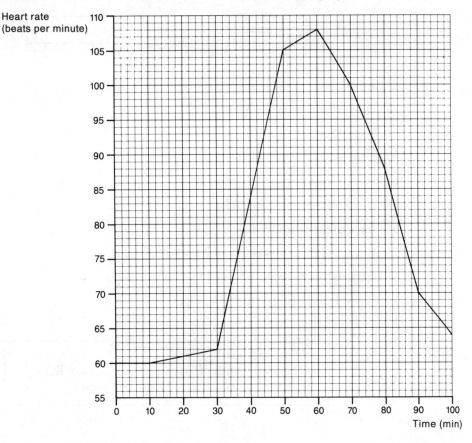

a) Using the information from the graph, complete the table of data below, showing the number of heartbeats at each of the time intervals.

Time (minutes)	0	10	20	30	40	50	60	70	80	90	100
Heart rate (beats per minute)											64

b) What is the heart rate at rest?

c) After how many minutes did the athlete

   i)   start the race?

   ii) stop running?

   Give a reason in each case.

d) Why did his heart rate increase just before he started running?

e) Give *two* reasons why the heart rate must increase during exercise.

10 Listed below are some properties of types of **blood vessel**. Separate them into three groups as follows:

Arteries	Veins	Capillaries

a) carry blood to the heart

b) carry blood from the heart

c) have thick elastic walls

d) have walls one cell thick

e) carry blood under high pressure

f) carry blood under low pressure

g) have thin muscular walls

h) oxygen and food pass through the walls

i) have valves to prevent back-flow

j) blood flows through them in pulses

> *Did You Know?*
> The total length of arteries, veins and capillaries in your body is about 100 000 kilometres!

11 a) Use the words from this list to complete the following passage about heart disease. (If necessary you may use a word more than once.)

> atheroma   beating   blocked   coronary   death   fatty
> heart attack   oxygen

The heart muscle receives blood from the _____ arteries. If one of these vessels becomes _____ the heart muscle in that area stops _____ because it is being starved of nutrients and _____. This is called a _____. It often occurs quite suddenly and is a very common cause of _____. Many factors contribute to heart disease, although the blockage itself is often caused by _____ material deposited in the _____ arteries. This is called an _____.

b) Below is a list of factors thought to be related to heart disease. For each one write one or two sentences which briefly explain how it contributes to the disease.

> diet   smoking   excess alcohol consumption
> lack of physical exercise   stress   obesity   high blood pressure
> inherited weakness   age

12 Copy the plan of the **circulation** below. Colour the arteries and the pulmonary vein red and the veins and the pulmonary artery blue.

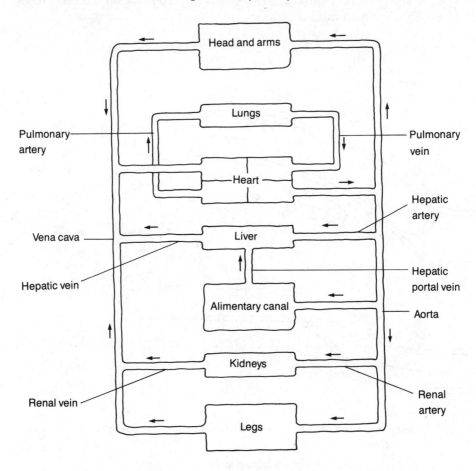

Using the letters A to J mark on your diagram the blood vessel which has

A   the highest pressure

B   the lowest pressure

C   the most oxygen

D   the least oxygen

E   the most carbon dioxide

F   the least carbon dioxide

G   the highest temperature when the body is resting

H   the most sugar after a meal

I   the least urea

J   the most urea

13 This question is about **tissue fluid formation**.

The diagram below shows the relationship between the cells, blood capillaries and lymph vessels.

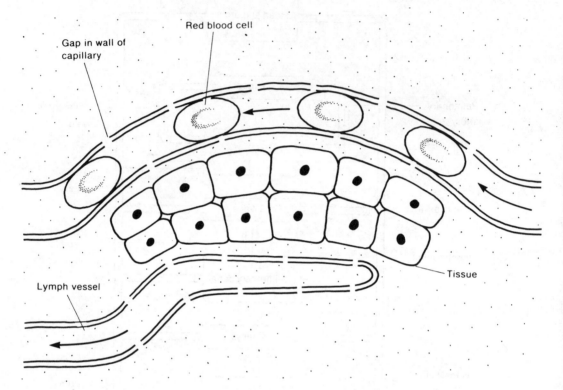

a) Copy the diagram and then label the points where you would expect to find:

   i)   the highest blood pressure

   ii)   the lowest blood pressure

   iii) fluid leaking out of the blood capillary

   iv)   fluid returning to the blood capillary

   v)   excess tissue fluid draining into the lymph vessel

b) Name:

   i)   *two* substances needed by the cells

   ii)   *two* waste substances produced by the cells

c) Why is tissue fluid formation essential for the normal functioning of cells?

d) Give *two* differences between blood and tissue fluid.

e) What eventually happens to the fluid draining into the lymph vessels?

12 **Photosynthesis**

1 a) Copy and complete the following passage about **green plants and the way they feed**:

The making of food by green plants is called _____ . This process uses _____ energy from the sun. This energy is trapped by the _____ in the leaves. The process also involves two raw materials, _____ from the air and _____ from the soil. Most of the food is made in the _____ of the plant. The most common kind of food they make is _____ . Green plants also make the gas _____ during this process.

b) Now complete the following equation, which summarises photosynthesis:

$$\text{................} + \text{................} \longrightarrow \text{................} + \text{................}$$
$$\text{(raw materials)} \qquad\qquad\qquad \text{(products)}$$

c) Copy and complete this diagram by filling in the empty boxes:

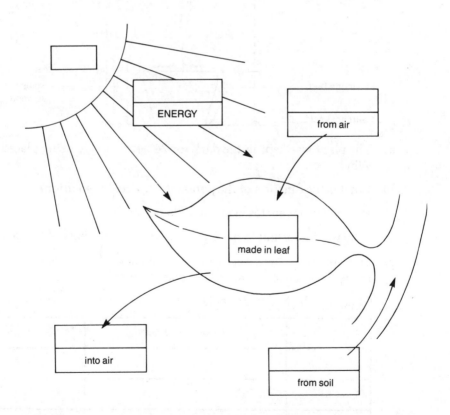

2 a) What precautions should you take when doing the starch test?

b) What colour will the leaf turn (at the end of the test) if starch is present?

3 Match the following pairs of statements and then place them in the correct order in which they occur:

Stages in the starch test   *Reason*

wash leaf in water   kills leaf

boil leaf in water   softens leaf

cover with iodine solution   removes chlorophyll

boil leaf in ethanol   stains starch

4 Study the diagram below and then answer the following questions.

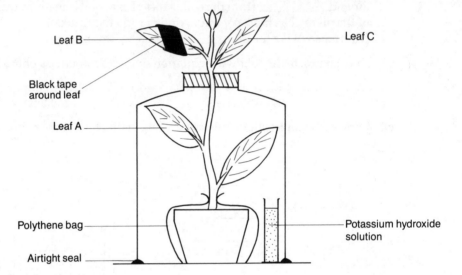

a) The plant was kept in the dark for 24 hours before being placed in sunlight. Why?

b) What is the function of the potassium hydroxide solution?

c) Why is the pot enclosed in a polythene bag?

d) Why is it important to have an airtight seal at the base of the bell jar?

e) The apparatus was set up as in the diagram and left for about twelve hours. Starch tests were carried out on the three leaves.

Complete the following table:

Leaf	*Result of starch test*	*Conclusion*
A		
B		
C		

f) Which one is the control leaf and why is it necessary?

5 a) What is unusual about leaf A below?

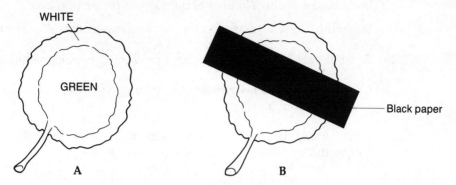

WHITE

GREEN

A

Black paper

B

b) How would you remove all the starch from a leaf?

c) Both the above leaves were destarched, then exposed to bright sunlight for six hours. If both leaves were then tested for starch in the usual way, what would they look like? Draw a diagram of each leaf to show the result.

d) What have you found out from this experiment?

e) Suggest *one* disadvantage to the plant of having leaves like this.

6 The diagram below shows an experiment that was carried out to measure how fast a water plant such as *Elodea* photosynthesises.

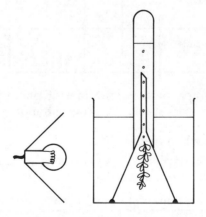

The shoot was exposed to different light intensities and the rate of photosynthesis estimated by counting the number of bubbles of gas leaving the shoot in a given time. The results are given below.

Number of bubbles per minute	7	14	20	24	26	27	27
Light intensity (arbitrary units)	1	2	3	4	5	6	7

a) Plot these data on a piece of graph paper, putting 'Light intensity' on the horizontal axis and 'Number of bubbles' on the vertical axis.

Study the diagram and the graph and then answer the following questions:

b) At what light intensity did the shoot produce 22 bubbles per minute?

c) Can you think of a better way of measuring the rate of photosynthesis than counting the bubbles?

d) What would be the effect of doing this experiment at the following temperatures? (*Clue*: Enzymes are involved in this process.)

i)   4 °C

ii)   30 °C

iii) 60 °C

e) What other factor can affect the rate of photosynthesis?

7 The information in the table below shows how the rate of photosynthesis varies with light intensity at two different carbon dioxide concentrations.

Light intensity (lux)	0	250	500	750	1000	1500	2500	4000	5500
Rate of photosynthesis (0.01% CO_2)	0	1.2	2.3	3.2	3.6	4.0	4.2	4.4	4.6
Rate of photosynthesis (0.1% CO_2)	0	1.8	3.5	5.0	6.1	8.1	11.4	13.7	14.8

a) Draw a graph to show the rate of photosynthesis (*y*-axis) against light intensity (*x*-axis) at each CO_2 concentration. Clearly label each curve.

b) Use the graph to predict
   i)   the rate of photosynthesis when the light intensity is 2000 lux and the CO_2 concentration is 0.1%
   ii) the lowest light intensity to produce a rate of photosynthesis of 12.

c) How do the graphs show that the rate of photosynthesis depends on
   i)   carbon dioxide concentration?
   ii) light intensity?

d) Use the graphs to explain what is meant by a limiting factor.

e) Name one other environmental factor which can limit the rate of photosynthesis.

8

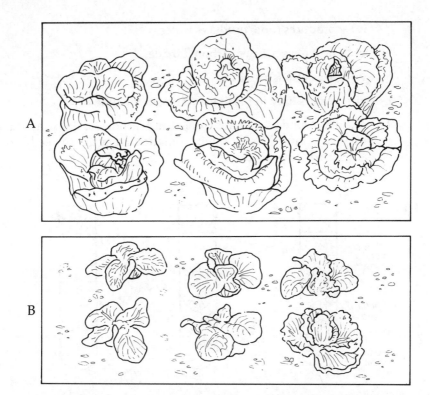

The diagram shows two batches of lettuce planted at the same time in an experiment to investigate the effect of carbon dioxide on growth. Batch A had had extra carbon dioxide added to the air around it.

a) Carefully explain the observed difference between the two batches.

b) Suggest three conditions which would have been kept constant during the experiment.

c) Lettuces can be commercially grown in large polythene tunnels. Suggest two advantages and two disadvantages of this.

d) Increasing the CO_2 levels used to grow crops costs money. What must a grower consider before deciding to do this?

9 a) Listed below are seven pairs of descriptions of respiration and photo-synthesis. Draw up a table and sort them into two groups:

Respiration	Photosynthesis

i) occurs in all cells/occurs in green plant cells

ii) energy is released/energy is stored

iii) produces carbon dioxide/produces oxygen

      iv)   produces food/produces water

      v)   uses oxygen/uses carbon dioxide

      vi)   uses water/uses food

      vii)   occurs only in the light/occurs all the time

b)   The air around us contains oxygen and carbon dioxide in amounts that do not vary very much. Using the information from the correctly completed table above, explain why this is so.

10

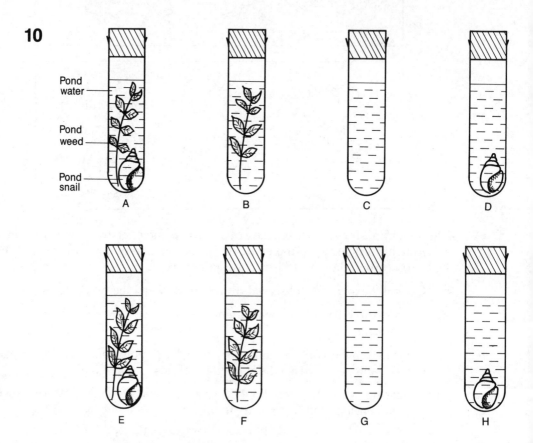

In an experiment, tubes A–H were set up as shown. Tubes A–D were kept in bright light for several hours. Tubes E–H were kept in the dark for the same length of time. Red bicarbonate indicator was then added to each test tube.

Bicarbonate indicator is used to show changes in carbon dioxide levels, which bring about a change in colour of the indicator.

Purple $\xleftarrow{\text{CO}_2 \text{ levels decrease}}$ Red $\xrightarrow{\text{CO}_2 \text{ levels increase}}$ Yellow

Bicarbonate indicator

a) Construct a table like the one below completing the results for each tube. (Tube C has been done for you.)

Tube	Respiration taking place?	Photosynthesis taking place?	CO₂ level unchanged, increased, or decreased?	Colour of indicator
C	X	X	Unchanged	Red

b) What effect does respiration have on carbon dioxide levels?

c) What effect does photosynthesis have on carbon dioxide levels?

d) Why were tubes C and G included?

e) Why were some tubes kept in the light and others in the dark?

f) In the light, photosynthesis proceeds at a faster rate than respiration. Which tubes show this? Explain your answer.

g) Why is the level of carbon dioxide in the atmosphere rising?

h) What is meant by the **greenhouse effect**, and why are scientists concerned about it?

11 Read the passage which is about **energy from biomass** and answer the following questions.

> With fossil fuels running out, the world needs renewable energy sources that can be re-made as fast as they are used up. Plant material called **biomass** is a good renewable energy source.
>
> Biomass energy is particularly important in developing countries, which often do not have their own fossil fuels and cannot afford to buy them. Examples of biomass fuels are wood, charcoal, alcohol, vegetable oil and biogas (methane).
>
> A tenth of the energy stored by the process of photosynthesis could provide all the world's energy needs.

a) What is the ultimate source of energy in the world?

b) What is a fossil fuel? Give an example.

c) What is a renewable energy source?

d) What is biomass?

e) Give *four* examples of biomass fuels.

f) Why is biomass energy particularly important in developing countries?

g) Why are tropical countries generally better able to produce biomass fuels than cool countries like Britain?

13 The Structure of Leaves

1 a) Make a large copy of the following diagrams about **leaves and their structure**:

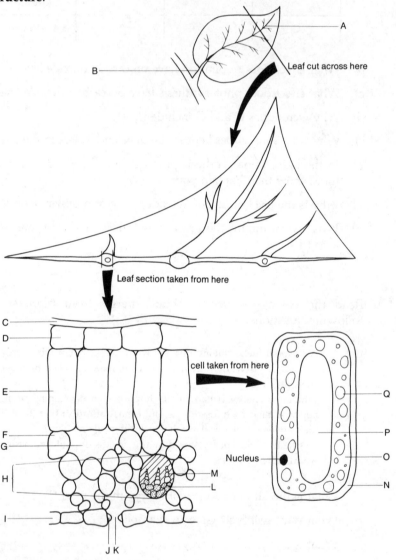

b) Replace the letters A to Q with the correct labels chosen from the list below:

air space   cell wall   chloroplast   cytoplasm   guard cell
lower epidermis   main vein (midrib)   palisade cell
petiole (leaf stalk)   phloem   side vein   spongy mesophyll cell
stomatal pore   upper epidermis   vacuole   waxy cuticle   xylem

2 Complete the following table by suggesting reasons for each of the observations about leaves:

Observation	Reason
Leaves have a large surface area.	
Leaves are often arranged so that they do not shade each other.	
Leaves have stomata.	
Leaves are thin.	
The upper epidermis is covered by a waxy cuticle.	
The mesophyll cells contain chloroplasts.	
The photosynthetic cells are mainly on the upper side of the leaf.	
There are air spaces between the mesophyll cells.	
The leaf contains transport tissue.	
Leaves contain starch.	

14 What Do Plants Need to Grow?

1 Study the diagrams and answer the questions.

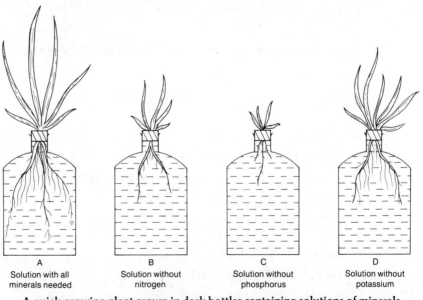

A	B	C	D
Solution with all minerals needed	Solution without nitrogen	Solution without phosphorus	Solution without potassium

A quick-growing plant grown in dark bottles containing solutions of minerals

a) Which plant shows the most growth, and why?

b) Describe one difference shown by plant A as compared with plants B, C and D.

c) During the experiment each bottle had air bubbled through it. Why was this necessary?

d) If a plant was grown in a solution without magnesium or iron, what would happen to the leaves, and why?

e) Why are the plants grown in dark bottles?

2 a) Copy the diagram below and add the following labels:

> cell wall   cytoplasm   vacuole   root hair   soil particle
> soil water   nucleus

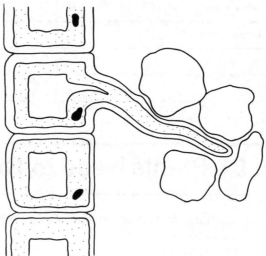

The diagram above represents part of a root in soil highly magnified.

b) How does water move from the soil into the root?

c) How do mineral salts enter the root cells?

3 Plants use the sugars that they make by photosynthesis to make all the other large complicated molecules that they need. Here are some examples:

> amino acids   cellulose   chlorophyll   starch

Which of these examples

a) is needed to make cell walls

b) acts as a food store

c) are needed to make proteins

d) is contained in chloroplasts?

15 Transport in Plants

1

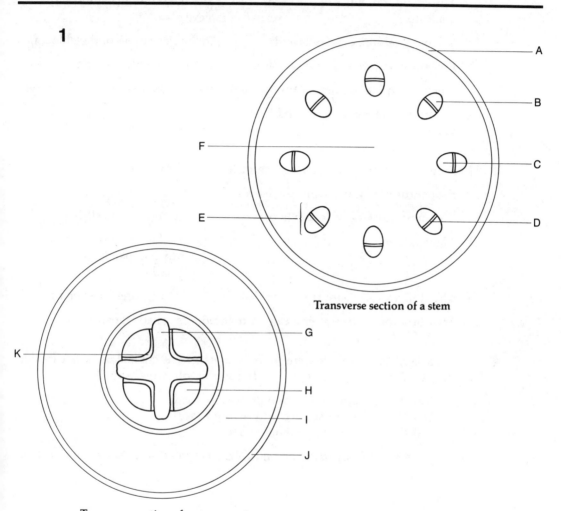

Transverse section of a stem

Transverse section of a young root

a) Copy the above diagrams and replace the letters A to K with the correct tissue name from the list below. (You may use some words more than once.)

   cambium   epidermis   packing tissue (parenchyma)   phloem
   vascular bundle   xylem

b) Suppose the sections above were taken from a plant that had had its roots placed for at least twelve hours in water containing a red dye. Shade on your drawing the areas that would appear red.

c) What differences can you see between the arrangement of **xylem** and **phloem** in the root and the stem? Suggest the reasons for this. (*Clue words:* support, flexible.)

2 Match the following phrases to make sentences. Each sentence should begin with the phrase on the left and finish with one of the phrases on the right.

a) **The vascular bundles of plants are made up of**   and they contain cytoplasm and sieve plates.

b) **Xylem vessels are dead cells and**   in the sieve tubes of the phloem.

c) **Phloem sieve tubes are living cells**   xylem and phloem tissues.

d) **Water and mineral salts are transported**   their walls are supported by lignin.

e) **Sugars are transported around the plant**   in the xylem vessels.

3 Here are some more phrases to match in the same way:

a) **Evaporation of water from the leaves**   by a waxy cuticle.

b) **The upper surface of leaves is covered**   by the guard cells.

c) **The epidermis is pierced**   by the size of the stoma, which depends on the guard cells.

d) **The stoma or air pore is surrounded**   by air pores or stomata.

e) **Transpiration from a stoma can be reduced**   is called transpiration.

4 Three leaves of the same size were cut from a plant. The cut end of each leaf-stalk was sealed. The leaves were then greased in the following way:

> leaf A – the upper surface only was greased
> leaf B – the lower surface only was greased
> leaf C – both surfaces were greased

All leaves were carefully weighed and then suspended in a warm room for six hours. They were then reweighed.

The results are given below:

	Mass immediately after greasing (g)	Mass after six hours (g)
Leaf A	5	3
Leaf B	5	4.5
Leaf C	6	6

a) For each leaf calculate the loss of mass.

b) Through which surface did the greatest water loss take place?

c) Name and draw the pore, and its surrounding cells, through which water evaporates.

d) What do the results tell you about the number of pores found on the upper and lower surfaces of leaves?

e) Why was the cut end of the leaf stalk sealed?

f) Why was it important to use leaves of the same size?

g) How could you measure the size (surface area) of a leaf?

5

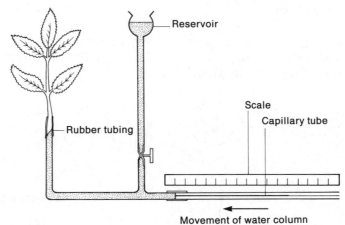

Movement of water column

A potometer

a) What does this apparatus measure?

b) In setting up a **potometer** give a reason for each of the following procedures:

   i)   The plant stem was cut under water.

   ii) The cut in the stem was diagonal and slanting.

   iii) Any drops of water on the leaves were removed with absorbant paper.

c) Give four conditions that would affect the rate at which a plant loses water (*Clue:* think of washing drying on a line).

d) How would you use the apparatus above to measure the rate of water loss?

e) Study the table below and then answer the following questions.

Conditions	The distance water moves along the capillary tube every two minutes (mm)
Cool, moving air, in light	100
Cool, still air, in light	30
Warm, moving air, in light	200
Warm, still air, in light	70
Warm, still air, in darkness	3

    i)   What is the function of the reservoir?

    ii) In which set of conditions did the plant lose water the most rapidly, and why?

    iii) In which set of conditions did the plant lose water the most slowly, and why?

  f) Give three reasons why the movement of water through a plant is helpful to the leaves.

6 An experiment to measure water loss by a potted plant was set up as shown below and left for several days near an open window. The loss in mass was recorded each day and the results are given below.

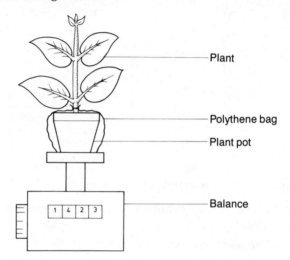

Day	1	2	3	4	5	6	7	8	9	10	11	12
Loss of mass (g)	4.2	4.8	5.4	7.0	4.6	8.5	6.0	3.2	4.8	4.6	4.6	4.8

  a) Using these results plot a graph to show the amount of water lost each day, putting 'Time (days)' on the horizontal axis and 'Mass (g)' on the vertical axis.

  b) Name the process by which a plant loses water through its leaves.

  c) Why was the pot covered with a polythene bag?

  d) Using these results, what do you think the weather conditions were likely to have been on

    i)   day six?

    ii) day eight?

    Give reasons for your answers.

  e) What control would you have used in this experiment?

7 Explain the following observations about plants and the way they adapt to various habitats:

a) Plants living in tropical rainforests tend to have large numbers of stomata on their leaves.

b) Desert plants sometimes have stomata set deeply into pits on the leaf surface.

c) Alpine plants are often covered in hairs.

d) Grasses living on sand dunes often curl their leaves.

e) Plants growing in arid areas often contain lots of woody fibres.

f) Plants growing in arid areas are often protected by a thick waxy cuticle.

16 The Kidney and Excretion

1 a) Make a *large* copy of the following diagram:

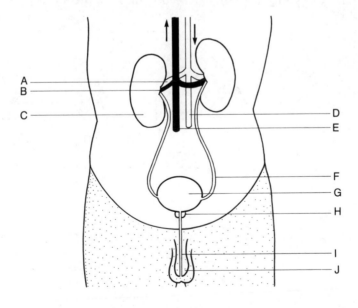

b) Replace the letters A–J with the correct label chosen from the list below.

aorta   bladder   kidney   penis   renal artery   renal vein
ring of muscle   ureter   urethra   vena cava

2 Now make a list of the above labels and for each one choose the correct function from the list below.

a) takes urine from the kidney to the bladder

b) prevents urine leaving the bladder

c) carries deoxygenated blood to the heart

d) removes urea from the blood

e) carries urine out of the body

f) also used during sexual intercourse

g) carries blood to the kidney

h) stores urine

i) carries blood away from the kidney

j) brings oxygenated blood from the heart

3 a) Copy this diagram of a section through **the kidney**:

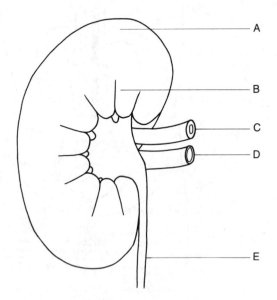

b) Replace the letters A–E with the correct label chosen from the list below.

cortex   medulla   renal artery   renal vein   ureter

4 Complete this passage about **the structure of the kidney** by filling in the missing words:

The kidney is composed of two main regions, the outer _____ and an inner _____ . Under a _____ many tiny nephrons can be seen: there are about one million in each kidney. Each nephron has a cup-shaped capsule at one end. This surrounds a small bunch of _____ called the _____ . Leading away from each capsule is a narrow _____ which twists and turns. This eventually joins a collecting _____ . These all lead to the _____ , which takes urine from the kidney to the _____ .

5 Copy the following simplified diagram of a **kidney nephron and its blood supply**. Explain what happens at each of the stages A to F, which show very simply how the nephron cleans the blood and makes urine.

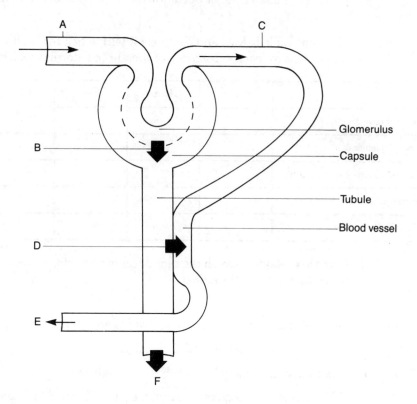

Now try to answer these questions as fully as you can:

a) Name the blood vessel that brings blood under high pressure to the kidney.

b) How is high blood pressure produced in the glomerulus?

c) What causes the fluid part of the blood to be forced through the walls of the capillaries into the space inside the capsule?

d) Which of the following

   i)   pass through the capillary walls?

   ii)   are too large to pass through the capillary walls and so stay in the blood?

     red blood cells   glucose   haemoglobin   urea   protein
     water   salt   white blood cells

e) As the fluid trickles along the tubule, all the glucose and some of the water and salt is taken back (reabsorbed) into the blood. Why is it important that this happens?

f) During some early work on diabetes it was noticed that ants were attracted to the urine of diabetic dogs. What was unusual about the dogs' urine? Doctors used to taste the urine of patients who were suspected of having diabetes. Why did they do this?

g) What is the main toxic or poisonous waste substance found in urine?

6 a) Copy the table below, and complete it with a tick for each substance present and a cross for each substance not present in a normal healthy person.

	Protein	Glucose	Urea	Water	Salt
Blood in renal artery					
Blood in glomerulus					
Fluid that passes into the capsule					
Urine leaving the kidney					
Blood in the renal vein					

b) Give *three* ways in which the blood leaving the kidney will be different from that which entered the kidney.

7 The diagram on the next page shows part of an artificial kidney machine.

a) Why is the tubing coiled and not straight?

b) What material is the tubing likely to be made of?

c) What process causes excess water in the patient's blood to pass into the dialysing fluid?

d) Name an excretory product other than water which will pass out of the blood into the dialysing fluid.

e) Where in the body is this excretory product made?

f) Why does this product pass from the blood in the coiled tubing into the dialysing fluid?

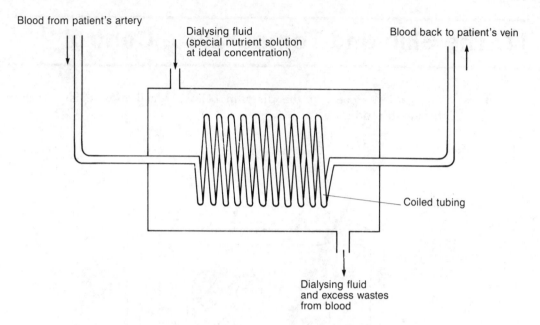

Blood from patient's artery

Dialysing fluid
(special nutrient solution
at ideal concentration)

Blood back to patient's vein

Coiled tubing

Dialysing fluid
and excess wastes
from blood

g) Name two nutrients present in the dialysing fluid.

h) Give two reasons why kidney transplantation is a better way of treating kidney failure than the use of a dialysis machine.

8 a) Complete this passage by choosing the correct word or words from inside the brackets:

After drinking several cups of tea or coffee the volume of the urine (increases/ decreases) and it looks (paler/yellower). The kidney is getting rid of excess (water/salt). On the other hand, on a hot day or after severe exercise the volume of urine (increases/decreases) and it looks (paler/yellower). This is called (excretion/osmoregulation).

b) Patients requiring dialysis by an artificial kidney machine must restrict their water and salt intake between dialysis sessions. Explain why.

17 The Skin and Temperature Control

1 a) Make a large copy of the diagram below, which represents a **section through the skin**.

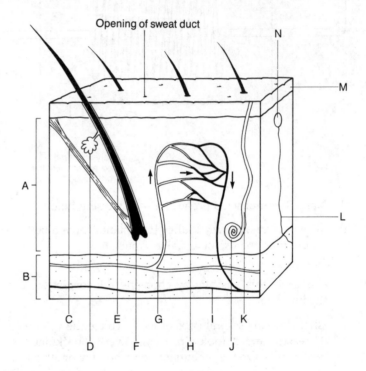

Opening of sweat duct

b) Replace the letters A–N with the correct label chosen from the following list:

artery   capillaries   dermis   epidermis   erector muscle
fat   hair   hair follicle   nerve   sebaceous (oil) gland
sense organ   sweat duct   sweat gland   vein

> *Did You Know?*
> In an average lifetime we shed about
> 20 kilograms of dead skin cells.

2 Consider the statements below about skin. Copy the following headings and then decide which statements belong under which heading:

Structure of skin	*Functions of skin*

a) The skin helps to protect the body from germs.

b) The skin contains a dark pigment called melanin in the Malpighian layer.

c) The skin can help to camouflage an animal.

d) The skin of mammals is covered in hairs.

e) The skin is waterproof.

f) The skin contains blood capillaries.

g) Scales of reptiles, feathers of birds and hairs of mammals all contain the protein keratin.

h) The skin helps to control body temperature.

i) Whales and seals have a thick layer of fat called blubber.

j) The skin is sensitive to stimuli.

k) The skin contains touch, pain, temperature and pressure receptors.

l) The skin contains sweat glands.

m) Melanin protects the body from ultraviolet rays.

n) The surface of the skin consists of dead cells.

o) Sebaceous glands open into hair follicles.

p) Sebaceous glands produce oil.

q) Erector muscles control hair movement.

r) Dead cells protect the skin from abrasion or rubbing.

s) Sweat consists mainly of salt and water.

t) Fat below the skin provides insulation.

3 Below are some phrases about **the skin and temperature control**. Consider each pair and decide which one goes into which column of the following table.

If it is cold	If it is hot

a) hairs lowered/hairs raised

b) erector muscle relaxes/erector muscle contracts

c) more air trapped between hairs/less air trapped between hairs

d) much heat lost/little heat lost

e) goose-pimples formed/no goose-pimples formed

f) surface blood vessels become narrower/surface blood vessels become wider

g) more blood flows to surface/less blood flows to surface

h) less heat radiates from skin/more heat radiates from skin

i) skin looks paler/skin looks redder

j) metabolic rate increases/metabolic rate does not increase

k) shivering occurs/shivering does not occur

l) sweat glands active/sweat glands inactive

m) heat lost by evaporation/no heat lost by evaporation

> *Did You Know?*
> If all your sweat glands were unravelled and joined together,
> they would reach a length of approximately 50 km.

4 The graph below shows how different species of mammals use up oxygen in respiration at different rates.

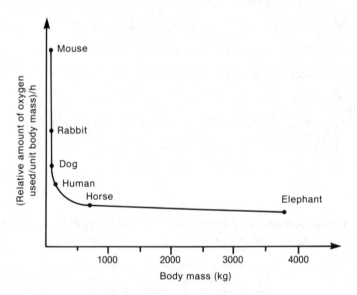

a) Study the pattern of the graph. What is the relationship between oxygen consumption and size?

b) What is the relationship between oxygen consumption and temperature control?

c) Why could a shrew starve to death in only a few hours, whilst a human could last for many days without food?

d) What is meant by the term **endotherm**?

e) What is the advantage of being an endotherm?

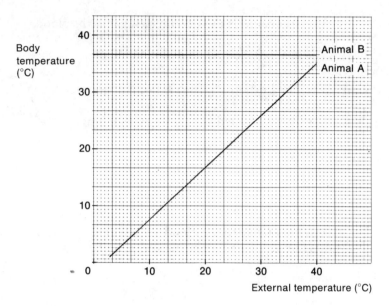

The graph shows how the body temperature of two different animals varies with the external temeprature.

f)   Which animal A or B is an endotherm? Explain your answer.

g)   Which of the animals could be a reptile? Explain your answer.

18 The Liver

1 Below are some statements about **the liver**. Consider each one and decide which statements are about:

Structure or position	Function

a)   The liver is the largest organ in the body.

b)   The liver produces bile.

c)   The liver detoxicates poisons.

d)   The liver has a rich blood supply.

e)   The liver produces a lot of heat.

f)   The liver stores glycogen.

g)   The liver is composed of millions of small cells.

h) The liver controls the amount of sugar in the blood.

i) The liver breaks down old red blood cells.

j) The liver breaks down excess protein to form urea.

k) The liver is situated just under the diaphragm.

l) The liver is a dark red colour.

2 This question refers to the **blood vessels that supply and drain the liver**. Study
the diagram below and then answer the questions.

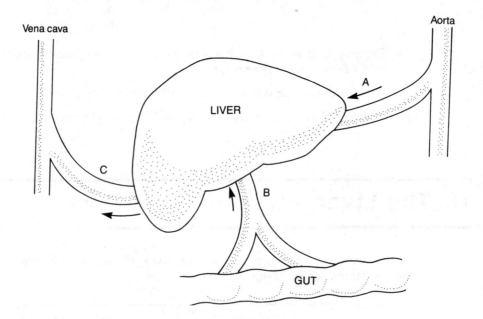

a) Identify each of the vessels A, B and C.

b) Then decide which vessel contains blood with
   i)   the highest oxygen content
   ii) the lowest carbon dioxide content
   iii) the highest temperature
   iv) the highest urea content
   v)   the highest amino acid content after a meal
   vi) the highest sugar content before breakfast

19 The Senses and Responding to Stimuli

1 Copy and complete this table about the **senses of the body**. Some of the gaps have already been filled in for you.

Names of sense receptor/organ	Where is it found in the body?	What is it sensitive to?	Energy change
Touch receptor	skin		
Pain receptor			
		hot and cold	
	tongue		chemical → electrical
	on the front of the head	light	
Ear			
	nose		
Semicircular canals			

> *Did You Know?*
> The skin contains about 4 million receptors sensitive to pain, temperature, pressure and touch.

2

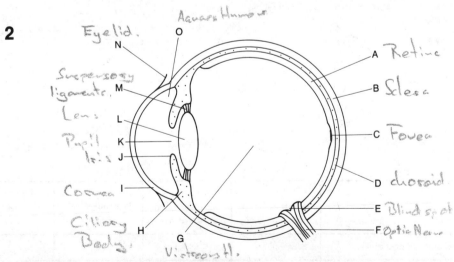

Make a large copy of the above diagram of **the eye** and replace the letters A to O with the correct label chosen from the following list:

aqueous humour   blind spot   choroid   ciliary body
conjunctiva   cornea   iris   lens   ligaments   optic nerve
pupil   retina   sclera   vitreous humour   yellow spot

> *Did You Know?*
> Your eyes are able to see nearly 8 million shades of colour.

3 a) Copy and complete the following table, putting a tick to mean yes, and a cross to mean no. For example, does the lens allow light to pass through? If yes put a tick; if no put a cross.

	Vitreous humour	Sclera	Lens	Blind spot	Pupil	Iris	Retina	Choroid	Cornea	Conjunctiva
Allows light to pass through	✓	✗	✓	✗	✓	✗	✗	✗	✓	✓
Bends or focuses the light rays	✗	✗	✓	✗	✗	✓				

b) Now write down the structures through which light passes in the correct order, starting at the front of the eye and finishing at the back.

4 Study the two diagrams below about **seeing things in focus** and then copy and complete the table.

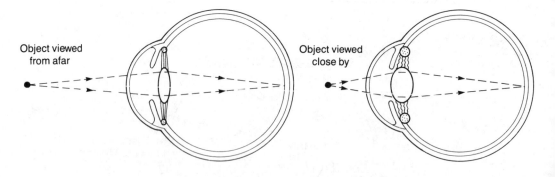

Object viewed from afar

Object viewed close by

	Is the lens round or flat?	Are the ciliary muscles relaxed or contracted?	Are the ligaments slack or tight?	Are the light rays bent a lot or a little?
When looking at near objects	round	✓	✗	lot
When looking at far away objects	flat	✗	✓	little

5 Match the following words and phrases to make correct sentences about **the eye and seeing**. Each sentence should begin with one of the phrases on the left and finish with one on the right. The first one has been done for you as an example:

The iris consists of . . . circular and radial muscles.

a)   **The iris consists of** ―― shape.

b)   **The retina contains** ―― messages to the brain.

c)   **The choroid contains** ―― dim light.

d)   **The yellow spot contains** ―― bright light.

e)   **The blind spot has** ―― circular and radial muscles.

f)   **The ligaments hold** ―― millions of light sensitive cells.

g)   **The pupil allows** ―― many blood vessels.

h)   **The cornea bends the** ―― only cones.

i)   **The lens can change** ―― no light-sensitive cells.

j)   **The optic nerve sends** ―― the lens.

k)   **The rods respond to** ―― light to enter the eye.

l)   **The cones respond to** ―― light rays.

cones light
sensitive.

> *Did You Know?*
> Your eyes have about 125 million rods and 7 million cones.

6 a)   Copy the passage below about **the eye and light** and fill in the gaps with words from the following list:

>   radial   larger   smaller   circular   relax(es)   contract(s)
>   less   retina

(Some words may be used more than once.)

In bright light the pupil becomes ___small___, owing to the action of the iris. The iris consists of _____ and _____ muscles. When one _____ the other _____. In bright light, the _____ muscles relax and the _____ muscles _____; thus the pupil becomes _____, allowing _____ light to fall on the _____ at the back of the eye.

> *Did You Know?*
> Your eye muscles move 100 000 times a day.

b) Copy the diagrams of the **iris** below. Replace the letters A–F with labels chosen from this list:

> **wide pupil in dim light**
> **narrow pupil in bright light**
> **circular muscles contracted**
> **circular muscles relaxed**
> **radial muscles contracted**
> **radial muscles relaxed**

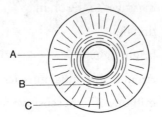 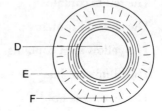

7 Complete this passage about **how we see**:

As light rays enter the eye they are bent by the _____ and the lens which focuses the light rays on to the _____. This contains light sensitive cells called _____ and _____. The image formed on the _____ is upside down and smaller than the object. The _____ and _____ are stimulated by light falling on them. Nervous _____ then pass along the _____ nerve to the _____ which interprets them.

8 a) Copy this diagram of the **human ear**:

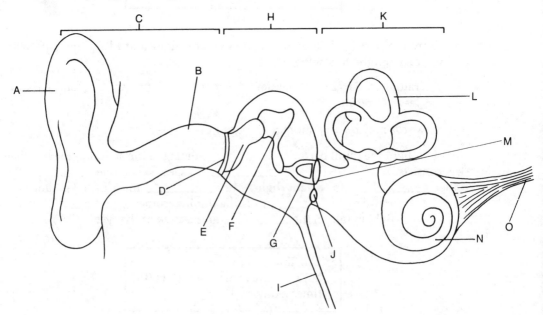

b)   Replace the letters A to O with the correct label chosen from the list below.

> anvil   auditory nerve   cochlea   ear-drum   Eustachian tube
> external ear channel   hammer   inner ear   middle ear
> outer ear   oval window   pinna   round window
> semicircular canals   stirrup

9   Consider the words following, which refer to either the eye or the ear (or both). Copy the headings below and then decide which word belongs under which heading:

The eye	The ear	Both

> sound   focus   retina   deaf   rods   light   frequency
> humour   blind   cones   loud   hammer   cochlea   pupil
> auditory nerve   soft   anvil   blind spot   iris   pinna
> dim   cornea   ear-drum   cataracts   wax   vibrate   lens
> Eustachian tube   oval window   round window   bright
> stirrup   pressure   optic nerve   conjuctiva

10   Complete the following table:

	Is it filled with air or fluid?
Outer ear chamber	
Middle ear chamber	
Inner ear chamber	

11   As sound passes through the ear, it comes into contact with the following structures:

> hammer   cochlea   stirrup   anvil   outer ear canal
> oval window   ear-drum   auditory nerve   brain   pinna

Starting with the pinna, place these structures in the correct order.

> *Did You Know?*
> There are more than 20 000 sensory hair cells in the cochlea.

12   Here are twelve sentences about **the ear and hearing**. The middle part of each sentence has been missed out. Choose from the list given the best word or words to complete each sentence. Some may be used more than once. (The first one has been done for you as an example.)

> **Two ears** . . . help to . . . tell us where sound comes from.

a)   **Two ears**   _____ tell us where sound comes from.

b) **The ear wax helps to** _____ dust and germs from entering the ear.

c) **The ear drum** _____ the outer and middle ear chambers.

d) **The three ear bones** _____ the sound vibrations.

e) **The Eustachian tube** _____ the back of the throat and the middle ear.

f) **The Eustachian tube** _____ the pressure on the ear drum.

g) **The oval window** _____ the middle and inner ear chambers.

h) **The cochlea** _____ fluid and sensory cells.

i) **Sensory cells** _____ vibrations of the fluid.

j) **Loud sounds can** _____ deafness.

> help to　　　prevent　　　connects　　　respond to　　　contains　　　cause
> balances　　　transmit and amplify　　　separates

13 Complete this passage about **how we hear**:

Sound waves are directed into the external ear canal by the _____. The waves cause the _____ to vibrate. The vibrations are magnified many times as they pass along the three tiny ear ossicles in the _____ ear chamber. The ossicles are called the _____, _____ and _____. The membrane covering the _____ window then vibrates and causes fluid in the cochlea to move. This stimulates tiny sensory hair _____. A nervous impulse is sent along the _____ nerve to the _____, which interprets the message and the sound is heard.

20 The Nervous System and Reflex Action

1 We respond to stimuli all the time.

a) Make a list of at least *six* stimuli to which you have responded in one day. Here are two examples to help you:

Stimulus	*Response*
I hear the telephone ringing	I pick up the receiver
I feel cold	I put on a pullover

b) Now think of some responses given by organisms other than humans. Write down several examples.

c) Match the following groups of words to make correct sentences about the nervous system. Each sentence should begin with the words on the left and finish with the words on the right.

The job of the nervous system	sensory and motor nerve fibres.
The central nervous system (CNS)	is to carry nerve messages around the body.
Nerves connect the CNS	little electrical pulses.
Nerve messages are	is composed of the brain and spinal cord.
Nerves are made up of	to all parts of the body.

> *Did You Know?*
> There are about 13 000 million nerve cells in your brain and nervous system.

2 a) Copy and complete the following sentences, filling in the missing words:

When our receptors are stimulated _____ nerve cells relay the message to the central nervous system. Here the _____ is sorted out. Messages are then relayed from the CNS to our muscles along _____ nerve cells.

b) Place the following words in the correct order:

response   **receptor**   **stimulus**   **effector**   **co-ordinator**

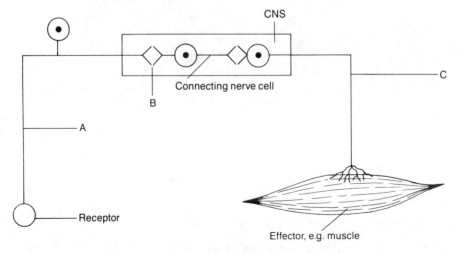

c) Copy the diagram above. Replace the letters A to C with the correct label chosen from the list below.

sensory nerve cell   **synapse**   **motor nerve cell**

Also on the diagram, use arrows to show the direction in which the message travels.

3 When we respond to stimuli, three things are needed:

   a) Sense organs, e.g. eyes, ears, etc. (*Clue words:* stimuli, detect)

   b) Nerves (*Clue word:* messages)

   c) Muscles or glands (*Clue words:* contract, move, bones, secrete)

Write down in sentences why each of these is important.

4 Look at this diagram about **reflex action**, and starting with number 1 match each of the numbers with one of the statements below. For example, 1 = pain receptors in the foot are stimulated.

   a) Impulse enters the spinal cord.

   b) Message is sent up the spinal cord to the brain.

   c) Pain receptors in the foot are stimulated.

   d) Message travels along sensory nerve cell.

   e) Message is received and sorted out by brain.

   f) Message travels along the motor nerve cell.

g) Foot is removed from the sharp stimulus.

h) Message leaves the spinal cord.

i) Muscles in leg and foot contract.

> *Did You Know?*
> Some nerve impulses can travel at about 240 kilometres per hour.

5 a) Copy the following diagram of a **reflex arc**:

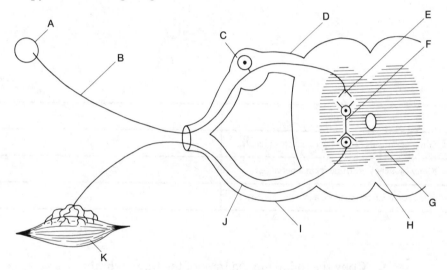

b) Replace the letters A–K with the correct label chosen from the list below.

> **dorsal root   ganglion   grey matter in spinal cord**
> **intermediate nerve fibre   motor nerve fibre   muscle   receptor**
> **sensory nerve fibre   synapse   ventral root**
> **white matter in spinal cord**

c) What would be the result if

i)   the dorsal root was cut?

ii) the ventral root was cut?

6 a) Copy the diagram of a motor **nerve cell** on the next page:

b) Replace the letters A–E with the correct label chosen from the list below.

> **axon   cell body   dendrites   myelin sheath   nucleus**

c)   For each of the features given in the table below suggest a reason.

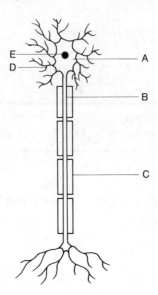

Feature	Reason
Some nerve cells can be over 1 metre in length.	
Many branches protrude from a nerve cell.	
The axon is surrounded by a layer of fat.	

7   a)   Copy the following diagram of the **human brain**:

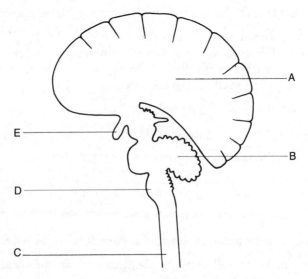

b) Replace the letters A–E with the correct labels chosen from the list below.

> cerebellum   cerebrum   medulla   pituitary gland   spinal cord

c) Which part of the brain is associated with each of the following functions?

  i)   balance and muscle movements

  ii) intelligence and memory

  iii) control of breathing and beating of the heart

Did You Know?
Your brain uses up about 25 per cent of the oxygen you breathe in.

---

8 Which of the following best describes what a drug is?

a) a substance that harms the brain

b) a substance that helps the body to fight infection

c) a substance that is addictive

d) a substance that alters the way the body works

9 Below are examples of drugs that affect the brain.

> cannabis   alcohol   opium   nicotine   morphine   caffeine
> barbiturates   sleeping pills   LSD   pep-pills   heroin   cocaine

Sort them into four groups under the following headings:

Sedative	Stimulant	Hallucinogen	Pain-killer

10 What is meant by drug abuse?

11 Read this passage about **heroin addiction** and then answer the following questions:

> Heroin was originally developed medically as a pain-killer, as a substitute for morphine, in the belief that it was less likely to produce addiction. The opposite has proved to be true. Heroin is one of the most addictive of all drugs. It is taken in various ways; it can be sniffed or smoked, but generally it is injected. In the early stages the needle is inserted just under the skin ('skin-popping'). The user will then progress to intravenous injection ('main-lining') by which stage he or she will have developed into an addict.
>
> Immediately after a dose of heroin the user experiences a state of sleepy well-being called euphoria. This fades quickly, passing into anxiety, agitation and constant worry about getting the next dose. With habitual use a heroin addict normally goes through successive stages of physical, mental and moral deterioration. The way of life of an addict is characterised by personal neglect – irregular and insufficient meals, insanitary habits and a disregard for hygienic precautions

during injections. Infections are common, e.g. abscesses and hepatitis. This neglect frequently leads to an early death, typically in the early thirties. The suicide rate among heroin addicts is said to be fifty times greater than it is in the general population. An addict who becomes pregnant may pass on the addiction to her baby. Immediate removal of the drug causes violent withdrawal symptoms which include sweating, convulsions, vomiting and diarrhoea. This is a painful and terrifying experience.

a) Why is it not desirable to use heroin medically as a pain-killer?

b) Briefly explain the following terms:

   addiction   euphoria   withdrawal symptoms

c) What is the difference between 'skin-popping' (line 5) and 'main-lining' (line 6)?

d) What is meant by 'physical, mental and moral deterioration' (line 11)?

e) What hygienic precautions should normally be taken before an injection?

f) What factors contribute to the early death of heroin addicts?

g) Why is withdrawal sickness known among addicts as 'the horrors'?

h) Addicts do not usually get pregnant because regular heroin injections tend to stop menstruation. Why might this be considered to be a fortunate effect?

21 Chemical Messengers

1 There are two types of **gland** in the body:

(A) glands with ducts   (B) ductless glands

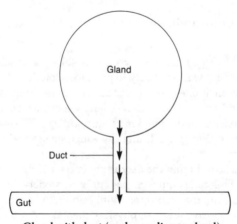

Gland with duct (such as salivary gland)

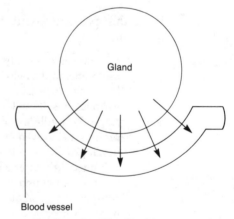

Ductless gland (endocrine organ such as adrenal gland)

Complete the table by naming the gland directly involved in each of these situations:

Situation	Glands with ducts	Ductless glands
a) Peeling onions		
b) A long walk on a hot day		
c) Feeling very tense before an exam		
d) Smelling mum's cooking		
e) Watching a sad film		
f) A mother breast-feeding her baby		
g) Laughing too much		
h) Watching a horror film		

2 Complete this passage by filling in the missing words:

Ductless glands produce _____ . There are no ducts or tubes, and so the products of these glands pass directly into the _____ .

3 Copy and complete this table. It is a summary of the human body's main ductless or endocrine glands and their secretions.

Gland	Hormone produced	Function
	Thyroxine	
		Prepares the body for action ('fight or flight')
Pancreas		
	Male sex hormones (androgens) (e.g. testosterone)	
	Female sex hormones (oestrogens and progesterone)	
	Growth hormone	

4 Copy the diagram of the human body and on it show the positions of the following glands:

    pituitary gland   **thyroid gland**   **adrenal glands**   **pancreas**
    ovaries   **testes**

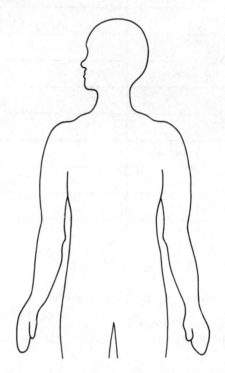

5 Some of the effects of the hormone **adrenalin** are listed below.

a) Copy the table and suggest a reason for each of the effects.

Effects of adrenalin	Reason
Breathing rate increases	
Heart beats faster	
More blood goes to brain	
More blood goes to muscles	
Less blood goes to skin and gut	
Pupil of the eye widens	
Blood sugar level rises	

b) Now in *one* sentence summarise the overall effect of adrenalin on the body.

6 The following statements are about **insulin, blood sugar and diabetes**. Copy and complete them by filling in the missing words.

a) Sugar is soluble and travels around the body in the _____.

b) Glycogen is insoluble and is stored in the _____.

c) Insulin makes the liver turn blood sugar into _____.

d) The disease diabetes is caused when the _____ fails to produce enough insulin.

e) The result is that the level of sugar in the blood _____.

f) Every day diabetics must inject themselves with _____.

7 Here are some questions about **diabetes**:

a) What would happen to the level of sugar in the blood if a diabetic

i) gave himself too much insulin?

ii) forgot to inject himself?

iii) ate three large bars of chocolate?

iv) missed the bus, had to run home and was late for tea?

b) Explain why each of the above would be dangerous.

c) Explain why injections of insulin are needed every day.

d) Suggest why the insulin might be less effective if it was taken in tablet form.

8 The nervous system and the endocrine system are both involved in controlling the internal environment.

Copy and complete the table below which compares the two systems.

Endocrine system	Nervous system
	Messages transmitted in the form of electrical impulses
Messages transmitted through the blood system	
Messages travel relatively slowly	
	The response is very quick
	The response is short-lived

9 Copy and complete the following diagram about the **control of blood sugar levels**.

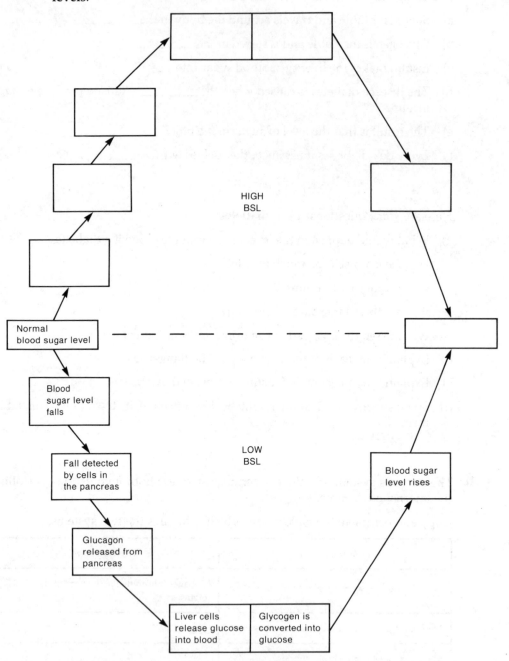

b) Explain how the fall in the level of glucagon as the blood sugar level returns to normal is an example of

   i)   homeostasis

   ii) negative feedback

22 How Plants Respond to Stimuli

1 Match the following groups of words to make correct sentences:

a)	**Plants and animals respond to**	quite quickly.
b)	**Animals usually respond**	changes in their environment.
c)	**Plants usually respond**	using their muscles.
d)	**Most animals move about by**	more slowly.
e)	**Plants are usually fixed**	tropisms.
f)	**Plants grow either towards**	geotropism.
g)	**Plant growth responses are called**	in one place.
h)	**A plant's growth response to light is called**	or away from a stimulus.
i)	**A plant's growth response to gravity is called**	phototropism.

2 Study the pictures below and then complete the table by putting a plus (+) if the shoot or root grows towards the stimulus and a minus (−) if it grows away from it.

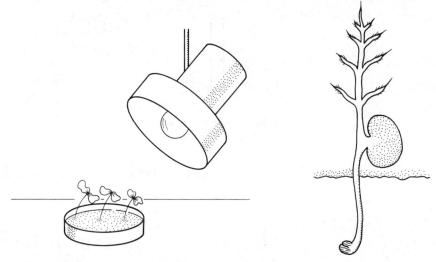

	Stimulus	
	Light	Gravity
Shoot		
Root		

3 Complete these sentences about tropisms by choosing the correct word or words from inside the brackets.

a) A shoot that grows (towards/away from) light is said to be positively phototropic.

b) A root that grows (towards/away from) light is said to be negatively phototropic.

c) A shoot that grows (towards/away from) gravity is called negatively geotropic.

d) A root that grows (towards/away from) gravity is called positively geotropic.

4

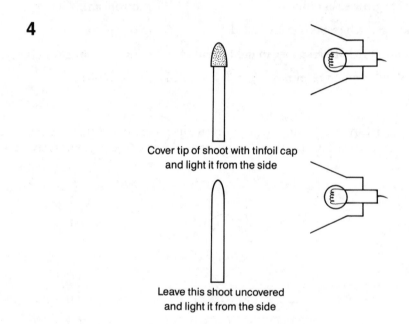

Cover tip of shoot with tinfoil cap
and light it from the side

Leave this shoot uncovered
and light it from the side

a) Study the diagrams above carefully. What would you expect to happen, and why?

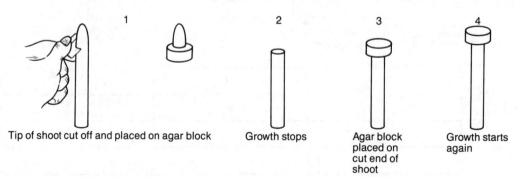

Tip of shoot cut off and placed on agar block   Growth stops   Agar block placed on cut end of shoot   Growth starts again

b) Look at the diagrams at the bottom of the previous page. What does this experiment tell you about the tip of the shoot and the part it plays in growth?

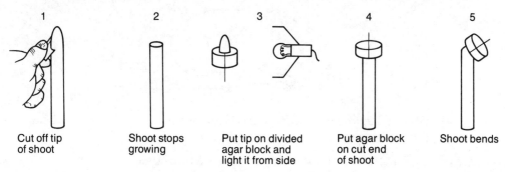

1	2	3	4	5
Cut off tip of shoot	Shoot stops growing	Put tip on divided agar block and light it from side	Put agar block on cut end of shoot	Shoot bends

c) Look at the diagrams above. How would you explain the results of this experiment?

5 Complete the following passage by filling in the missing words:

The _____ of the shoot produces a hormone called _____. This hormone causes cells behind the tip to _____. When the shoot is lit from one side, more _____ gathers on the dark side. Therefore the cells there grow _____ and the shoot bends _____ the light.

6 The response to gravity is often studied with an instrument called a clinostat. It consists of a drum which rotates slowly. Seedlings are pinned to a piece of cork on the drum as shown below.

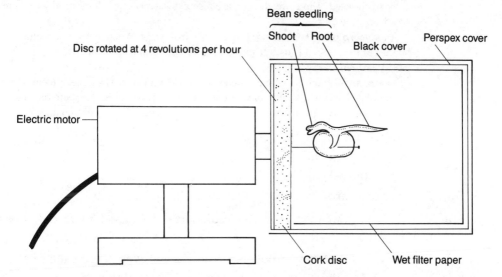

a) Draw the appearance of the *root* after 3 days.

b) Carefully explain why your bean seedling has grown in this way.

c) Why must experiments like this be done in the dark?

7 Here is a diagram of a bean seedling whose shoot and root have been marked at regular intervals:

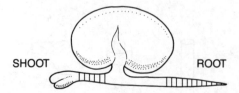

SHOOT   ROOT

a) Draw a diagram to show how this bean seedling would look after being left in this position for 3 days.

b) Explain the reason for its appearance after this time.

8 Read the passages below which are about **the use of growth regulators** in plants. Answer the questions which follow each one.

> The main function of plant hormones is to control growth. It is therefore hardly surprising that these hormones or similar chemicals made by Man, have been extensively used in crop production. Auxins are a group of hormones which have been isolated from a large number of different plants. **Synthetic auxins** are used as **selective weedkillers**. When sprayed onto crops they have a greater effect on broad-leaved plants than on the narrow-leaved ones. The growth of the broad-leaved plants is so severely disrupted that they die, while the narrow leaved plants at most suffer a temporary reduction in growth. As most of Man's cereal crops are narrow-leaved and the weeds which compete with them are broad-leaved, such selective weedkillers are extensively used. These weedkillers are also extensively used domestically to control weeds in lawns.
>
> Another synthetic auxin is used to increase fruit yield. When it is sprayed onto some species of fruit tree, it causes fruit to develop without the need for fertilisation. This is called **parthenocarpy**.
>
> Auxins are also the active ingredients of rooting powders. The development of roots is stimulated when the ends of cuttings are dipped into these compounds. Another plant hormone can be used to stimulate ripening of citrus fruits and tomatoes.

a) Explain what is meant by
  i) a synthetic auxin?
  ii) a selective weedkiller?
  iii) parthenocarpy?

b) Why do you think that selective weedkillers have a greater effect on broad-leaved plants?

c) Explain why selective weedkillers are used extensively by cereal farmers.

d) Why do gardeners use rooting powder?

> One of the best known selective weedkillers is 2,4,5-trichlorophenoxyacetic acid (2,4,5-T). In its production an impurity called **dioxin** is formed. Dioxin is one of the most toxic substances known to Man: a single gram is enough to kill more than 5000

humans. Even in minute quantities it may cause cancer, a skin disorder called chloracne and abnormalities in unborn babies. Dioxin was a constituent of a **defoliant** called Agent Orange used by the Americans in the Vietnam war. Fifty million litres of it were sprayed over jungle areas to cause the leaves to drop so that enemy camps would be revealed. The dioxin produced physical and mental defects in children born in the area and to those born to American servicemen who were there when it was used. In 1976, an accident in Seveso, Italy, resulted in the release of dioxin into the atmosphere.

e) How is dioxin formed?

f) What is a 'defoliant'?

g) What conditions are likely to have been suffered by people who were living close to the factory at Seveso?

h) Hormones can be used by humans to control various processes.

Copy and complete the following table which considers the various benefits and problems associated with hormone use:

Hormone use	Benefits	Problems
Stimulating root growth in cuttings		
Promoting fruit development		
Killing weeds by disrupting their normal growth pattern		
Increasing growth for meat production		
Increasing milk production		
Stimulating egg release from ovaries		
Inhibiting egg release from ovaries		

9 Many plants are sensitive to touch; some also depend on touch to catch insects. Here are some examples. Using a library, try to find out as much as you can about these unusual plants.

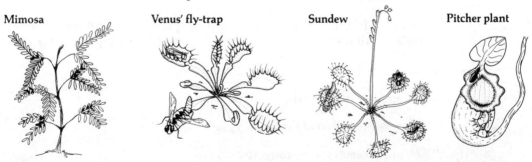

Mimosa   Venus' fly-trap   Sundew   Pitcher plant

23 The Skeleton and Movement

1 On the next page are some sentences to do with the **skeleton**. The middle part of
each sentence has been missed out. Choose from the list below the best word or
words to complete each sentence. Some may be used more than once. (The first one
has been done for you as an example.)

The body . . . is protected by . . . the skeleton.

a) **The skeleton**   _____   the soft organs of the body.

b) **Blood cells**   _____   inside some bones.

c) **The skeleton**   _____   muscles to bring about movement.

d) **The skeleton**   _____   bone.

e) **Bone**   _____   calcium.

f) **Calcium**   _____   bones hard.

g) **Gristle**   _____   cartilage.

h) **Tendons**   _____   muscles to bones.

i) **Ligaments**   _____   bones to bones.

j) **The skull**   _____   the brain.

k) **The ribs**   _____   breathing.

l) **The rib cage**   _____   the heart and lungs.

m) **A moving joint** _____   lubricating fluid.

> contains   protects   are made   is made of   makes   connect
> help in   works with   is protected by

2 Study this list of bones, and using a labelled diagram of a human skeleton answer
the questions below:

> skull   femur   humerus   ribs   pelvis   vertebrae   ulna
> tibia   fibula   radius   pubis   patella   carpals   tarsals

a) Which of the above bones are found in the legs and feet?

b) Which ones are found in the arms and hands?

c) Which ones are joined to the breast bone?

d) Which one protects the reproductive organs?

   e) Which ones surround the nerve cord?

   f) Which one is fused to the backbone for strength?

> *Did You Know?*
> Each of your hands has 27 bones, your spine has 26
> and your skull 21.

3 Here are some more questions about the skeleton for you to try:

   a) Why are pregnant women encouraged to drink milk?

   b) Why do women usually have broader hips than men?

   c) Why is the femur so much larger and stronger than the humerus in humans?

   d) Why are X-rays used to see if a bone is broken?

   e) Why do you think motor cyclists have to wear crash helmets by law?

4 Study this diagram of the **arm**:

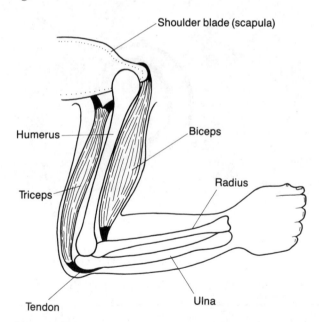

Complete the following passage by choosing the correct word or words from
inside the brackets.

When you bend your arm at the elbow the following things happen:
The biceps (contracts/relaxes), becoming (shorter and fatter/longer and thinner).
The triceps muscle (contracts/relaxes), becoming (shorter and fatter/longer and
thinner). When you straighten your arm the (same/opposite) happens. The
(triceps/biceps) muscle will do work when a weight is lifted off the ground.

5 Complete this table about **joints** and their position in the body:

Joint	Bones on either side of joint	Type of joint: hinge or ball and socket
Hip		
Shoulder		
Elbow		
Knee		
Jaw		

> *Did You Know?*
> There are over 100 joints in your body and about 650 different muscles.

6 Copy the diagram below, which represents a **moving joint**.

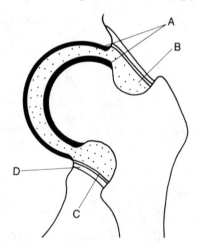

a) Replace the letters A to D with the correct labels.

b) Next to your diagram copy and complete this table:

	Name of structure	Function
A		
B		
C		
D		

7 Explain what is meant by the following:

a) a sprain

b) a dislocation

c) a fracture

Theme 5

The Continuity of Life

1 Producing Offspring

1 Complete the following sentences by choosing the correct word or words from inside the brackets.

a) Asexual reproduction (involves/does not involve) the production of male and female sex cells.

b) Sexual reproduction (involves/does not involve) the production of male and female sex cells.

2 Write down *one* advantage and *one* disadvantage of asexual reproduction.

3 Match each of the following with one of the definitions below:

> gamete   egg   sperm   fertilisation   viviparous   hermaphrodite
> zygote   embryo   metamorphosis

a) Male sex cell

b) An organism that produces both male and female sex cells

c) A change in form from larva to adult

d) The joining of male and female sex cells

e) A fertilised egg develops into this

f) Organisms which give birth to live young

g) Female sex cell

h) The biological name for a sex cell

i) A fertilised egg

4 Write down *one* advantage and *one* disadvantage of sexual reproduction.

5 Explain the difference between internal and external **fertilisation**.

6 Give the names of *three* animals that are hermaphrodite.

7 Complete this diagram:

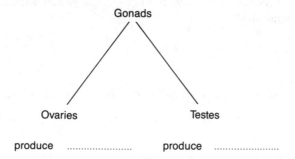

Gonads

Ovaries   Testes

produce ....   produce ....

8 Use labelled diagrams to show the structure of a human egg and a human sperm.

9 Complete the following table which describes four ways in which an egg differs from a sperm:

Feature	Egg	Sperm
Size		
Shape		
Food store		
Movement		

10 Use labelled diagrams to show how fertilisation takes place.

2 Reproduction in Insects

1 Choose the correct word or words from inside the brackets to complete these sentences:

a) All insects reproduce (sexually/asexually).

b) The eggs are fertilised (externally/internally).

c) The male insect passes sperms into the body of the female during a process called (mating/egg laying).

d)   Insect eggs are often laid close to a supply of (warmth/food).

e)   The female locust lays her eggs in the (water/sand) to protect them from the
     (wind/sun).

2 Copy and complete these sentences about how insects develop:

a)   Insects that develop gradually show _____ metamorphosis. An example
     is _____ .

b)   Insects that undergo a complete change in their life cycles show _____
     metamorphosis. An example is _____ .

3 Explain the meaning of the following words:

             moulting   mating   metamorphosis

4 This diagram shows the life cycle of a butterfly:

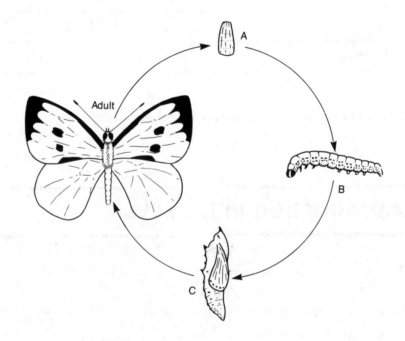

a)   Copy the diagram and complete it by replacing the letters A, B and C with the
     names of the three stages.

b) Which stage in the life cycle is concerned with
   i)   increasing population size?
   ii)   increasing the size of the individual?
   iii) surviving the winter months?
   iv)   metamorphosis?
   v)   spreading the population to new areas?

   In each case explain your answer.

c) Copy and complete the table below.

Feature	Survival value
Larva Powerful cutting jaws Soft expandable cuticle Poisonous hairs or warning colours	
Pupa Dull coloured Few if any signs of movement Usually found in dry sheltered places	
Adult Distinctive colours and patterns on wings Complex antennae Feed on nectar	

d) This diagram represents the life cycle of the house-fly. Copy the diagram and complete it by filling in the two missing stages D and E.

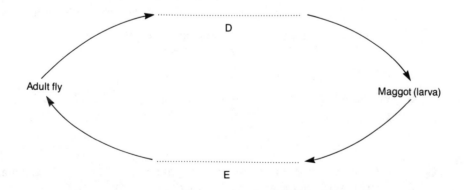

e) Do the life cycles of the butterfly and house-fly show complete or incomplete metamorphosis? Explain your answers.

5 This diagram shows the life cycle of the locust:

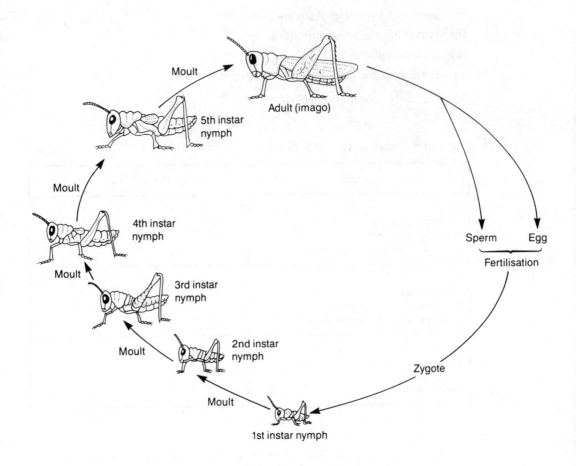

a) Write a short description of the locust life cycle. Include the following words:

   adults   mating   egg laying   hatch   nymph   moults
   wing buds   sex organs   instar

b) Why are locust nymphs called hoppers?

c) Why can locust nymphs grow in size only by moulting?

6 a) What is the advantage of an insect egg hatching into a larva (e.g. a maggot or a caterpillar) rather than a small adult?

   b) A woman planted a bush with brightly coloured, sweet-scented flowers, to attract butterflies to her garden. However, she planted it very close to her vegetable patch. Why was this a mistake?

3 Reproduction in Vertebrates

There are five classes of vertebrates. You should be able to think of examples of animals in each class. All of them reproduce sexually but there are differences in the way that the eggs and sperms are brought together, and in the way the young develop.

1   Copy and complete this table:

	Do they reproduce in water or on land?	Is fertilisation internal or external?	Do they lay eggs or are they viviparous?	Do the eggs have shells?
Fishes				
Amphibians				
Reptiles				
Birds				
Mammals				

2   Study this table and then answer the questions:

Animal	Number of eggs produced per year	Where eggs are laid
Cod	9 000 000	water
Frog	10 000	water
Turtle	1000	sand
Penguin	8	land

a)   Write down *two* reasons why fish lay so many eggs.

b)   Why does a frog lay fewer eggs than a cod, even though they both lay their eggs in water?

c)   Why do penguins lay fewer eggs than turtles?

3 These diagrams show stages in the life history of a frog. Look at them and answer the questions.

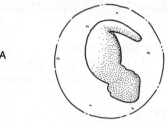

A

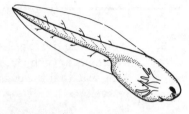

B

Frog spawn. The tadpole is ready to emerge from the jelly.

Three days after hatching from the jelly

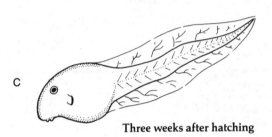

C

D

Three weeks after hatching

An adult frog

a) What is the function of the jelly in the frog-spawn in diagram A?

b) What food is eaten by each of the stages?

c) How do stages B, C and D obtain oxygen from the water?

d) What changes occur between stages C and D?

e) Write down *three* reasons why amphibians need water to reproduce.

4 a) When birds (e.g. robins) reproduce they usually perform a series of actions, one after the other. Put the following sentences in the order in which they occur.

   The birds build a nest.
   The female incubates the eggs.
   The male claims a territory.
   The female lays her eggs in the nest.
   The parents look after the chicks.
   The male's song attracts the female.
   The eggs hatch.
   The two birds mate.

b) Why are courtship displays important in birds' reproduction?

c) Why is it an advantage to a pair of breeding birds to have their own territory?

d) How do feathers help birds to produce their offspring successfully?

5 Draw and label two diagrams:

a) to show the internal structure of a bird's egg just after fertilisation

b) to show the developing embryo inside an egg

6 a) Copy and complete this table by filling in the functions of the different parts of a bird's egg:

Parts of a bird's egg	Function
Porous shell	
Yolk	
Albumen (white)	
Air space	
Dense twisted albumen	

b) Before boiling an egg many people prick the shell at the blunt end. Why is this a good idea?

4 Human Reproductive Systems

1 Copy this diagram of the human **female reproductive system**. Replace the letters A to F with labels chosen from this list:

cervix   opening of vagina   ovary   oviduct   uterus   vagina

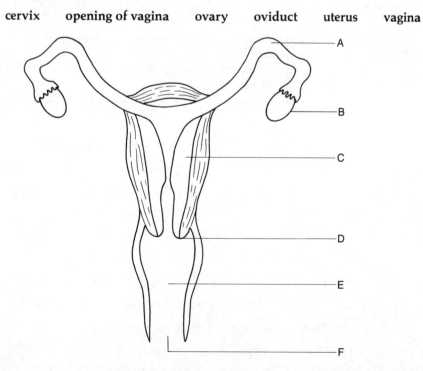

2 Copy this diagram of the human **male reproductive system**. Replace the letters A to H with labels chosen from this list:

> epididymis   penis   prostate gland   scrotum   seminal vesicle
> sperm duct   testis   urethra

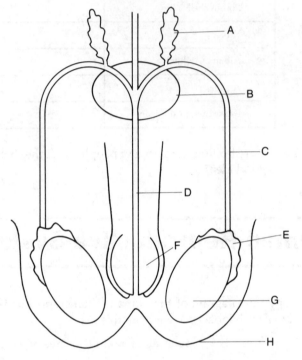

> *Did You Know?*
> There are over a kilometre of sperm-producing tubes in each testis.

3 Write down these names of organs of the female reproductive system:

> ovaries   oviducts   womb   cervix   vagina

Below each one, write down the correct descriptions of the organ from the following list:

a) The neck of the womb.

b) Its biological name is the uterus.

c) There is one on each side of the abdomen.

d) It connects the womb to the exterior.

e) They connect the ovaries to the womb.

f) The organ in which eggs are produced.

g) A pear-shaped organ with a muscular wall.

h) The place where fertilisation occurs.

i) The place where sperms are deposited during intercourse.

j) They are also called the Fallopian tubes.

k) The place where the baby develops.

l) One egg is released from here about every 28 days.

4 Write down these names of organs of the male reproductive system:

**testes   scrotum   epididymis   sperm ducts   seminal vesicle
prostate gland   penis**

Below each one, write down the correct descriptions of the organ from the following list:

a) There are two of them.

b) They are long coiled tubes.

c) It is the loose sac of skin that contains the testes.

d) They connect the testes to the urethra.

e) The urethra runs though this organ.

f) It produces fluid which helps the sperms to swim vigorously.

g) It contains large numbers of blood vessels.

h) The organ in which sperms are made.

i) They are suspended in the scrotal sac.

j) The place where sperms are stored.

k) It becomes erect during intercourse.

l) They are made up of a large number of tiny tubules.

Did You Know?
The average adult male produces approximately
300 million sperms each day.

---

5 Correctly match the words in the left-hand column with the definitions in the right-hand column.

Words	Definitions
Words	*Definitions*
ovulation	the release of semen from the penis
semen	the release of an egg from an ovary
ejaculation	the transfer of sperms into the female's body
fertilisation	the sinking of a fertilised egg into the lining of the uterus
implantation	the fluid containing sperms
copulation	the time when the egg is fertilised
conception	the joining of an egg with a sperm

6 Mark on your diagram of the female reproductive system

a) where fertilisation occurs

b) where implantation occurs

c) where sperms are deposited during intercourse

7 About 200 million sperms are contained in the semen which is ejaculated during intercourse. Why are there so many?

5 Human Sexual Development and the Menstrual Cycle

1 Which of the following is the best definition of puberty?

a) The time when a girl's periods start

b) The period between the ages of 11 and 16

c) The time when sex organs become active and secondary sexual characteristics develop

d) The time when you become more interested in members of the opposite sex

e) The time when a child becomes an adolescent

2 Answer these questions about sexual development in males:

a) Write down *three* changes that occur in a boy's body at puberty.

b) Which hormones bring about these changes?

    c)   Where are these hormones produced?

    d)   At about what age do these changes usually occur?

3 Answer these questions about sexual development in females:

    a)   Write down *four* changes that occur in a girl's body at puberty.

    b)   Which hormones bring about these changes?

    c)   Where are these hormones produced?

    d)   At about what age do these changes usually occur?

    e)   What is the menopause and approximately when does it occur?

4 Match the days of the menstrual cycle in the left-hand column with the events in the right-hand column.

Approximate Days of Cycle	Events
1–5	ovulation
6–12	yellow body breaks down
13–15	menstruation
16–25	Graafian follicle develops
26–28	yellow body develops

5 Choose words from the list to complete the sentences below about the menstrual cycle. Each word should be used only once.

> **Graafian**   **ovulation**   **oestrogen**   **egg**   **immature**
> **progesterone**   **womb**   **fertilised**   **unfertilised**   **follicle**
> **corpus luteum**

    a)   During menstruation the lining of the _____ breaks down.

    b)   The ovaries contain thousands of _____ eggs.

    c)   A single egg develops inside a _____ follicle.

    d)   The follicle produces a hormone called _____.

    e)   On about day fourteen of the cycle _____ occurs.

    f)   The empty _____ develops into a yellow body.

    g)   The yellow body is also called a _____.

    h)   The yellow body produces a hormone called _____.

    i)   If the egg is _____ the yellow body withers away.

    j)   If the egg is _____ the yellow body remains.

    k)   One of the ovaries releases an _____ every month.

6 What is incorrect about these two statements?

a)   The menstrual cycle is 28 days long.

b)   Ovulation occurs two weeks after menstruation begins.

7 If ovulation occurs on the fifteenth day of the menstrual cycle and sperms can survive inside the female for three days and an egg can live inside the Fallopian tube for two days, on which days of the cycle could sexual intercourse result in pregnancy?
(It is important to remember that ovulation does not always occur fifteen days after the start of a period.)

6 Pregnancy and Birth

1 Complete the following sentences, choosing the best word or words from those in the lists:

a)   When an egg is fertilised it divides to form a ball of cells called an . . .

i)   amnion.

ii)   embryo.

iii)   foetus.

iv)   ovum.

b)   Pregnancy begins when . . .

i)   an egg is released from the ovary.

ii)   intercourse takes place.

iii)   an egg is fertilised.

iv)   a fertilised egg sinks into the lining of the uterus.

c)   A baby develops inside the . . .

i)   Fallopian tube.

ii)   ovary.

iii)   uterus (womb).

iv)   vagina.

d) After about two months of development the embryo looks like a miniature human being and is called . . .

   i)   an amnion.

   ii)   a foetus.

   iii) a placenta.

   iv) the uterus.

e) The foetus is surrounded by a thin membrane called the . . .

   i)   amnion.

   ii)   placenta.

   iii) umbilicus.

   iv) uterus.

f) The foetus is cushioned by the . . .

   i)   placenta.

   ii)   mother's blood.

   iii) amniotic fluid.

   iv) umbilical cord.

g) The foetus gets its food and oxygen from the mother's blood through the . . .

   i)   amnion.

   ii)   embryo.

   iii) amnionic fluid.

   iv) placenta.

h) The waste products that pass from the foetus into the mother's blood include . . .

   i)   oxygen and urea.

   ii)   faeces and urea.

   iii) carbon dioxide and urea.

i) The important hormones produced by the placenta during pregnancy are . . .

   i)   oestrogens and progesterone.

   ii)   oestrogens and insulin.

   iii) adrenaline and progesterone.

j) The time between conception and birth is called . . .

i)   the conception period.

ii)   the gestation period.

iii) the menstrual period.

k) Conception is the time when . . .

i)   an egg is released.

ii)   an egg is fertilised.

iii) an embryo becomes a foetus.

l) In humans pregnancy lasts for approximately . . .

i)   20 weeks.

ii)   30 weeks.

iii) 40 weeks.

2 a) What is usually the first sign of pregnancy?

b) What should a woman do when she first thinks that she is pregnant?

3 Copy the diagrams below. Replace the letters A to H on both diagrams with labels from this list:

    amnion   amniotic fluid   cervix   embryo   foetus   placenta
    umbilical cord   wall of uterus

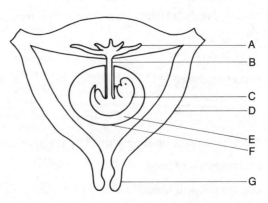

An embryo in the uterus about 4 weeks old

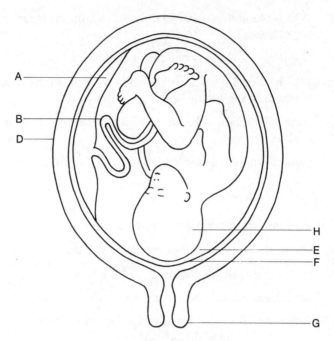

A

B

D

H
E
F

G

A foetus in the uterus just before birth

4 Look carefully at this diagram, which shows the relationship between the blood system of the foetus and that of the mother, and then answer the questions:

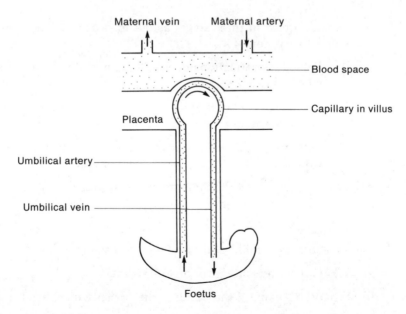

Maternal vein   Maternal artery

Blood space

Capillary in villus

Placenta

Umbilical artery

Umbilical vein

Foetus

a) Copy the diagram above.

b)   Which blood vessel carried blood, rich in waste products, from the foetus to the placenta?

c)   Name *two* of these waste products.

d)   Which blood vessel carries blood, rich in food and oxygen, from the placenta to the foetus?

e)   Name *three* food substances which must be supplied to the foetus to ensure healthy growth.

f)   How do these substances pass across the placenta?

5 Give reasons why a pregnant woman should

a)   attend an ante-natal clinic regularly during her pregnancy

b)   not smoke or drink alcohol

c)   not take any medicines unless told to do so by the doctor

d)   have been immunised against German measles (rubella)

e)   pay regular visits to the dentist

f)   drink about a pint of milk a day

g)   eat a well balanced diet

h)   wear low-heeled shoes

6 a)   Labour occurs in three stages as outlined below. Put them in the order in which they occur.

   i)   Powerful contractions of the uterus push the baby through the vagina, usually head first.

   ii)   The uterus contracts at regular intervals more and more powerfully. The cervix opens and the water sac bursts.

   iii)   Relatively mild contractions of the uterus force the placenta to come away from the wall of the uterus and pass out through the vagina.

b)   Why is it important for babies to cry as soon as they are born?

7 Babies require only milk for the first few weeks of their life.

a)   What are the advantages of breast-feeding?

b)   What is the name of the glands in the breasts which secrete the milk?

c)   How are babies provided with food before they are born?

8 a) Decide which of the statements below apply to identical **twins** and which ones apply to non-identical twins. Organise your answer in table form.

     i)   They are formed from a single fertilised egg which splits in two.

     ii)   They are formed from two separate eggs, fertilised by two different sperms.

     iii)   They each have their own placenta.

     iv)   They share the same placenta.

     v)   They are always of the same sex.

     vi)   They may be of the same sex or different sexes.

     vii) They are also known as fraternal twins.

     viii) They each have the same genes.

     ix)   They are only as alike as any brothers or sisters.

     x)   They sometimes develop as Siamese twins.

b) Draw diagrams to show how identical and non-identical twins are produced.

7 Preventing Pregnancy

1 What is a contraceptive?

2 The following are the most common methods of contraception:

       the sheath   the cap or diaphragm   spermicides   the pill
       the rhythm method

Answer these questions about the different methods:

a) Which methods prevent sperms reaching an egg?

b) What is a spermicide?

c) Which method or methods do not require a doctor's examination and supervision?

d) How can the reliability of the sheath and the diaphragm be improved?

e)   How does the pill prevent pregnancy?

f)   What is an intra-uterine device?

g)   Which method is used by the man?

h)   Which method is the most reliable?

i)   Which method is the most unreliable? Explain why.

j)   Which method could be described as safe, reliable, easily obtained and easily used?

k)   Which method also gives protection against sexually transmitted diseases such as AIDS and gonorrhea?

3 a)   How is sterilisation carried out in

   i)   males?

   ii)   females?

b)   Which is the simpler and safer of the two operations?

c)   When might a couple decide that sterilisation is the best way of preventing pregnancy?

4 Why is family planning a good thing for

a)   married couples?

b)   children?

c)   the world?

5 Does family planning always involve contraception? (What about people who find it difficult to start a family?)

6 Where can people go for family planning advice?

7 The diagram shows the human female reproductive organs.

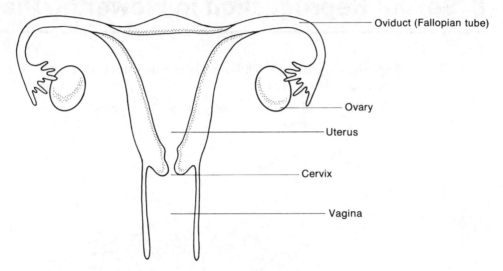

a) Explain why a woman with blocked Fallopian tubes cannot get pregnant in the normal way.

b) Read the following passage and, with the help of the diagram, answer the questions below.

> A woman with blocked Fallopian tubes can now have a 'test-tube baby'. She is given hormones to increase the number of eggs maturing in each ovary. A doctor, using a fine tube through the body wall, searches for and sucks up several eggs from the surface of the ovary just before they are released naturally. The eggs are put in a culture solution in a dish. Semen containing sperm is added and fertilisation usually occurs. Three days after fertilisation, embryos of between eight and 16 cells have formed. Two or three of these embryos are gently transferred by a fine tube via the cervix into the uterus. If the process is successful, at least one of the embryos develops into a baby.

   i) Suggest why the doctor wants to increase the number of eggs maturing in each ovary.

   ii) Suggest why the doctor wants to collect eggs just before they are released naturally and at what stage of the menstrual/oestrous cycle the doctor would do this.

   iii) Suggest features of the culture solution which are essential for a successful test-tube baby.

   iv) What is 'fertilisation'?

   v) Suggest why the doctor waits three days before transferring the embryos to the uterus.

   vi) Suggest why, when embryos are put in the uterus, the tube is passed through the cervix and not through the body wall.

c) Do you think the term 'test-tube baby' is a good one? Give reasons for your answer.

8 Sexual Reproduction in Flowering Plants

1 a) Copy this diagram of a wallflower in section. Replace the letters A to H with labels from the following list:

anther   filament   ovary   ovule   petal   receptacle
sepal   stigma

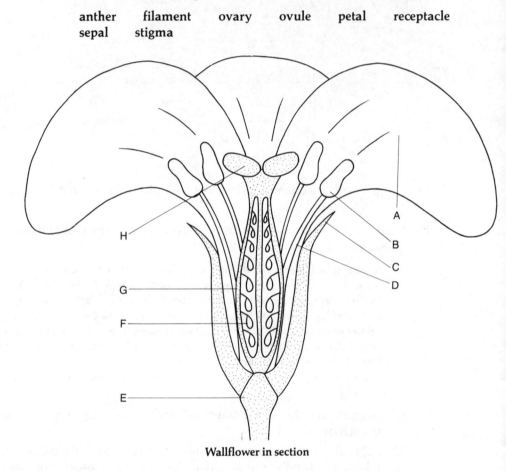

Wallflower in section

b) The wallflower is pollinated by insects. Which parts of the flower have the function of attracting insects?

2 Match the parts of a flower in the left-hand column with their correct functions in the right-hand column.

Parts of a Flower	Function
receptacle	to support the anther
style	to produce pollen
stigma	to make a sugary liquid
pollen	to receive pollen

petal   to contain the male gamete
nectary   to attract insects
sepal   to form the base of the flower
anther   to hold up the stigma
ovary   to protect the flower in bud
filament   to contain the female gametes

3 Copy and complete these two sentences:

a) The transfer of pollen from the anther to the stigma is called _____ .

b) The joining of the male nucleus from the pollen grain with the egg cell in the ovule is called _____ .

4 Explain each of the following:

a) Wind-pollinated flowers do not have brightly coloured petals, do not have nectaries and are not scented.

b) The stamens of wind-pollinated flowers hang outside the petals. The anthers are loosely attached to the filaments.

c) The stigmas of wind-pollinated flowers are often feathery and hang outside the petals.

d) The pollen grains of wind-pollinated flowers are very light and are produced in vast numbers.

e) The pollen grains of insect-pollinated flowers have spikes.

5 The inflorescence of a grass is made up of many small wind-pollinated flowers.

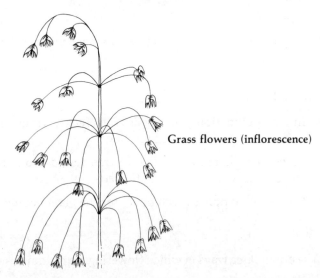

Grass flowers (inflorescence)

a) What is an inflorescence?

b) Copy this diagram of a single grass flower. Replace the letters A to G with labels chosen from this list:

anther   filament   ovary   pollen grains   stamen   stigma

style

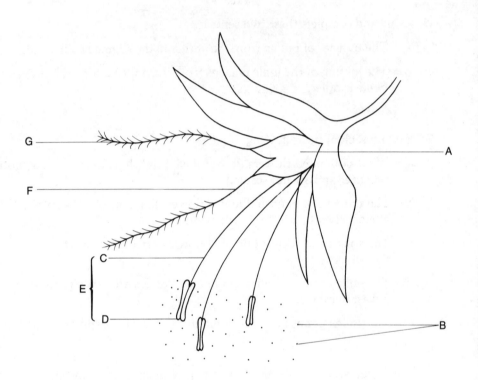

c) What features of this flower help to make wind pollination successful?

6 Copy and complete these sentences:

a) In self-pollination, pollen is transferred from the _____ to the _____ of the _____ flower.

b) In cross-pollination, pollen is transferred from the _____ to the _____ of a _____ flower.

c) Cross-pollination is much better for the plant because it creates _____.

7 Write down *three* ways in which flowering plants can ensure cross-pollination.

8 a) Copy this diagram of a **carpel** (the female part of a flower). Replace the letters A to F with labels chosen from this list:

   egg cell   **micropyle**   **ovary**   **ovule**   **stigma**   **style**

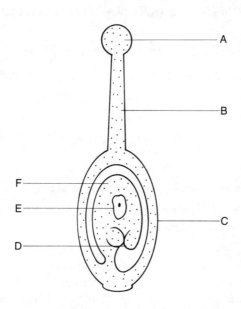

b) Complete the diagram to show how a pollen grain, once it has landed on the stigma, fertilises the ovule.

9 Copy and complete this table to show what happens to the flower parts after fertilisation:

Flower parts	What happens after fertilisation
Petals	wither away
Sepals	
Stamens	
Egg cell	
Ovule	
Ovary	

9 Fruits and Seeds

1 Complete these sentences about **seeds** by choosing the correct word from inside the brackets:

a) Fruits and seeds are formed from the (flowers/leaves).

b) When seeds are dried out they are said to be (dormant/dead).

c) When they are (dead/dormant) seeds can survive summer drought and winter cold.

d) Broad bean seeds are found inside fruits called (shells/pods).

2 This question is about the **structure of seeds**.

a) Match the word or words in the left-hand column with the descriptions in the right-hand column.

seed coat (testa)	the young shoot
embryo	protects the seed
plumule	stores food
radicle	consists of plumule and radicle
seed leaf (cotyledon)	the young root

b) Copy this diagram of half a broad bean seed. Replace the letters A to E with labels from this list:

plumule   radicle   embryo plant   seed coat   seed leaf

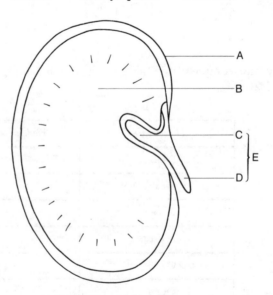

Half of a dormant broad bean seed

c)   If you took a dry broad bean seed and soaked it, what differences would you expect there to be between the dry and the soaked seed? How can you explain them?

d)   Complete this passage by choosing the correct words from inside the brackets:

If iodine solution is placed on the seed leaves of a broad bean, they will turn (yellow/black) because they contain (sugar/starch) which will feed the (embryo/seed) when it starts to grow.

3   These questions are about the **germination** of the broad bean seed.

a)   Copy this passage about the germination of a broad bean seed but include only the correct word from inside the brackets.

Before germination the broad bean seed must take in (food/water) mainly through a tiny hole called the (testa/micropyle). This causes the seed to (swell/ shrivel) and the seed coat bursts open. The (embryo/seed leaf) starts to grow. The young (root/shoot) appears first and grows (downwards/upwards). The young (root/shoot) appears next and grows (upwards/downwards). Eventually the (root/shoot) breaks through the surface of the soil. The first green (leaves/flowers) appear. The young plant is called a (seedling/embryo).

b)   i)   Copy this diagram of a bean seedling:

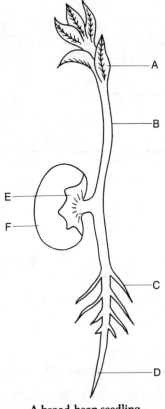

A broad bean seedling

Replace the letters A to F with labels from this list:

**first green leaves   main root   side root   seed coat
seed leaf   stem**

ii)   Mark the position of the surface of the soil on your diagram.

c)   Complete this passage:

The carbohydrate food required for germination of a broad bean is _____ and it is stored in the _____ . Enzymes change this insoluble substance into soluble _____ which can be transported to the tips of the _____ and _____ where growth takes place. Once the seedling has formed its first _____ it can _____ its own food by _____ .

4 a)   Name *three* conditions required for seeds to germinate.

b)   This experiment was set up to investigate the conditions required for germination.

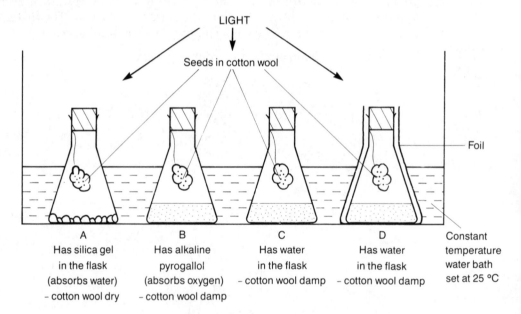

A	B	C	D	Constant
Has silica gel in the flask (absorbs water) – cotton wool dry	Has alkaline pyrogallol (absorbs oxygen) – cotton wool damp	Has water in the flask – cotton wool damp	Has water in the flask – cotton wool damp	temperature water bath set at 25 °C

i)   Will the seeds germinate in each of the flasks A, B, C and D? Give detailed reasons for your answers.

ii)   How could you extend the experiment to show that warmth is necessary for seeds to germinate?

5 a)   What is meant by seed dispersal?

b)   Write down *two* advantages to a plant of having its seeds dispersed away from the parent plant.

6 The following are drawings of fruits. Copy them and next to each one write down an explanation of how seed dispersal is brought about. The dandelion has been done for you as an example.

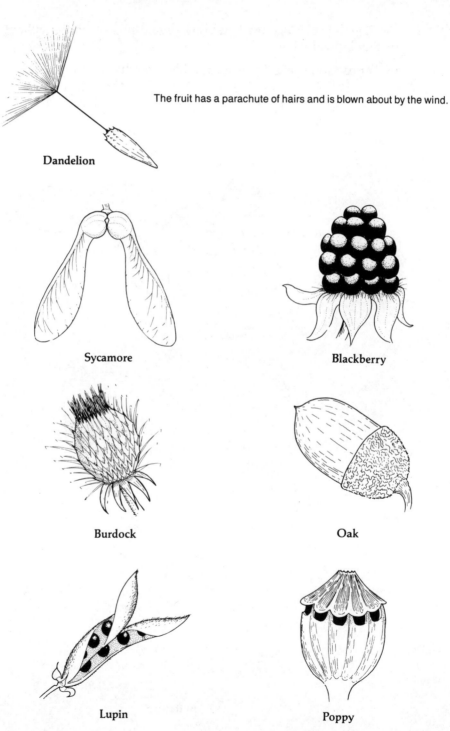

The fruit has a parachute of hairs and is blown about by the wind.

Dandelion

Sycamore

Blackberry

Burdock

Oak

Lupin

Poppy

10 Reproduction without Sex

1 The diagrams below show how some organisms reproduce without the help of another individual.

a) For each one describe the method of reproduction involved.

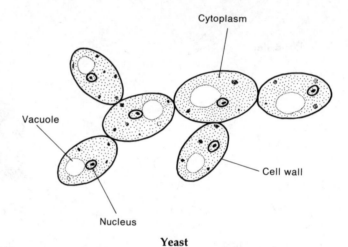

Cytoplasm

Vacuole

Nucleus

Cell wall

Yeast

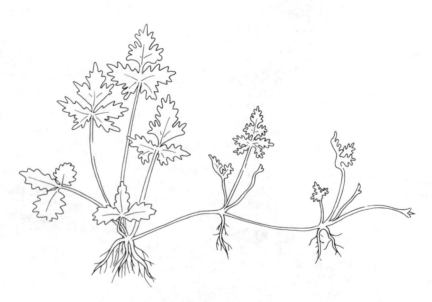

Buttercup

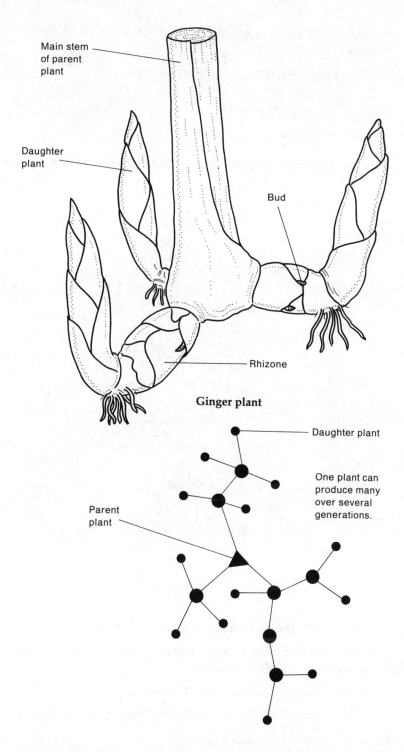

Main stem of parent plant

Daughter plant

Bud

Rhizone

Ginger plant

Daughter plant

One plant can produce many over several generations.

Parent plant

b)   What terms are used to describe this form of reproduction?

c)   Explain why all the offspring produced in this way are identical.

d) What conditions are usually needed for this type of reproduction to take place?

e) When might this type of reproduction be

    i)   an advantage

    ii)   a disadvantage

    to the ginger plant?

2 Study the diagram of a potato plant in July and answer the following questions:

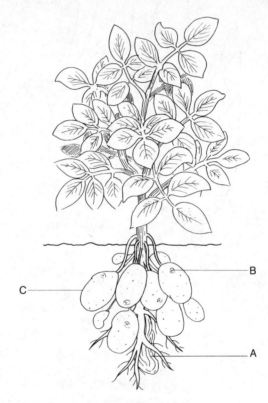

A potato plant in July

a) Explain why the structure A is in a shrivelled condition at this time of year.

b) Assuming that all the tubers develop, how many new plants will this plant produce in the following spring?

c) What would be likely to develop from structure B?

d) Explain why all the new plants will be identical to the original plant.

e) Food is stored in structure C.

    i)   What type of food is stored?

    ii)   What chemical test would show the presence of this food?

iii)   Where and how is the stored food made?

iv)   How are the food products transported from the place where they are made to the tubers?

v)   What happens to the stored food when the tubers start to develop in the spring?

vi)   Why is the potato plant so important to humans?

3 a) By using labelled diagrams, explain how gardeners may reproduce plants by the following methods:

   cuttings   layering   grafting and budding

b)   Why do gardeners carry out the processes of grafting and budding?

c)   What are the advantages and disadvantages of vegetative reproduction

   i)   to the plants?

   ii)   to the gardener?

4 Read the passage below which is about **cloning plants**. Answer the questions which follow.

> A clone is a group of genetically identical organisms. They can be produced using asexual methods of reproduction. Many plants are produced in this way using techniques such as layering, budding and grafting. Recently a new cloning technique has been developed called **tissue culture**. Carrot plants were the first to be cloned.
>
> Using **sterile techniques** a tiny piece of stem is cut from a carrot seedling. This is put onto **nutrient agar** in a petri dish. The cells of the stem **divide mitotically** to form a clump of cells called a callus. These cells can be separated and each one grown into a new carrot plant.
>
> Much research is being carried out into cloning economically important plants. **High yielding** varieties of the oil palm (used in the production of margarine, soaps and detergents) have been successfully cloned but it took scientists at Unilever ten years to develop the tissue culture techniques required. The possibility of cloning Norway Spruce trees which are resistant to acid rain is being investigated.

a)   Describe two methods of cloning plants without using tissue culture.

b)   Explain the meaning of each of the following as used in the passage:

   i)   genetically identical
   ii)   sterile techniques
   iii) nutrient agar
   iv)   divide mitotically
   v)   high yielding

c)   Explain why the carrot plants, produced by the method described in the passage, form a clone.

d) Oil palms can be grown from the seeds collected from high yielding varieties. Why do you think Unilever spent so long looking for a way to clone the plants?

e) Why are Norway Spruce trees of economic importance?

Scientists have discovered that they can also produce animals by cloning. One way is to remove the nucleus from an unfertilised egg and replace it with a nucleus from a body cell. The egg cell with its new nucleus can then grow into a new individual.

f) How will the amount of genetic material differ between the nucleus which has been removed and the one which has replaced it?

g) Early cloning experiments were done on the eggs of frogs and toads. Why was this easier than using the eggs from rabbits and sheep?

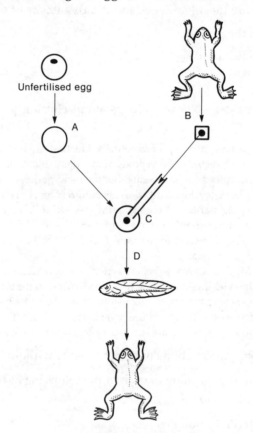

h) Copy the simplified diagram above about **how to clone a frog**. Explain what happens at each of the stages A–D.

i) Which parent will the cloned frog look like? Explain your answer.

j) Suggest, with your reasons, *one* advantage and *one* disadvantage of cloning farm animals.

11 Growth

1 Read the following statements, which are about growth. Some of them are true, and others are false. Choose the correct statements and write them down.

a)   Cell division is an important part of growth.

b)   Mature organisms grow at the same rate as young ones.

c)   A growing organism needs plenty of food.

d)   Growth is a characteristic of all living things.

e)   Energy is not required for growth.

f)   Many organisms grow more quickly in warm conditions.

g)   Height is the best way of measuring growth.

h)   In growing animals cell division usually takes place all over the body.

i)   In young plants cell division takes place mainly at the tips of shoots and roots.

j)   Growth is best defined as a permanent increase in biomass.

2 An organism's rate of growth can be estimated by measuring its height, length, volume, mass, girth or area. For each of the following suggest *two* ways of measuring the growth rate:

a)   tadpole

b)   mouse

c)   man

d)   oak-tree

e)   bean seedling

f)   locust

3 Some information on the growth of a sunflower stem is given in the table below.

Age (days)	7	14	21	28	35	42	49	56	63	70	77	84
Height (cm)	16	34	62	98	135	172	206	228	247	251	254	255

a) Draw a graph of these results. Label the axes as shown.

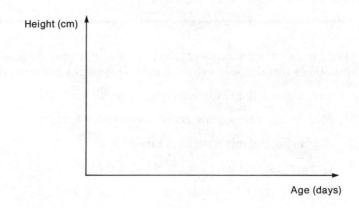

This is a **growth curve**.

b) Describe the shape of the growth curve.

c) What is the length of the stem after

i)   10 days?

ii)   30 days?

iii)   46 days?

iv)   80 days?

d) When is the stem growing

i)   most rapidly?

ii)   most slowly?

4 Some information on the growth of a hamster is given in the table below.

Age (days)	3	6	12	28	38	48	66	110	160	200
Mass (g)	3	4	10	30	54	76	92	102	106	107

a) i)   Draw the growth curve from this information.

ii)   How many *weeks* did it take the hamster to become an adult?

b) Make a list of *four* factors that might affect growth.

c) Draw on the same axes the growth curve you would expect if the hamster was given less food.

d) Draw the growth curve for a fish from the information in this table:

Age (years)	1	2	3	4	5	6	7	8
Mass (g)	10	60	145	225	300	360	400	420

e) How does the growth curve of the fish differ from that of the hamster?

5 Some information on the growth of a human baby *before* birth is given in the table below.

Age (months)	0	1	2	3	4	5	6	7	8	9
Length (cm)	0	1	4	9	16	25	30	34	38	42

a) Draw the growth curve from this information.

b) When is the baby growing

  i) most rapidly?

  ii) most slowly?

6 The table below shows the average heights of boys and girls up to the age of 18.

Age (years)		0	1	2	3	4	5	6	7	8	9
Average height (cm)	Boys	51	75	87	96	103	110	117	124	130	135
	Girls	50	74	87	96	103	109	116	122	128	133

Age (years)		10	11	12	13	14	15	16	17	18
Average height (cm)	Boys	140	144	150	155	163	168	172	174	174
	Girls	139	145	152	157	160	161	162	162	162

a) Draw the two growth curves (one for boys and one for girls) on the same graph.

b) In what respects are the curves

  i) similar?

  ii) different?

c) When does the most rapid growth take place?

d) When does growth slow down?

e) At what age are girls generally taller than boys?

7 Pea seeds were planted in soil in seed boxes and given suitable conditions for
germination. Twenty seedlings were removed each week, washed to remove any
soil and then heated in an oven to 110 °C, until all the water had been removed.
The batches of dry seedlings were then weighed to determine their mass. The
results are shown below.

Age (weeks)	1	2	3	4	5	6	7
Dry mass of twenty seedlings (g)	6	4	2	1	8	25	45

a) Plot a graph of these results. Label your axes as shown.

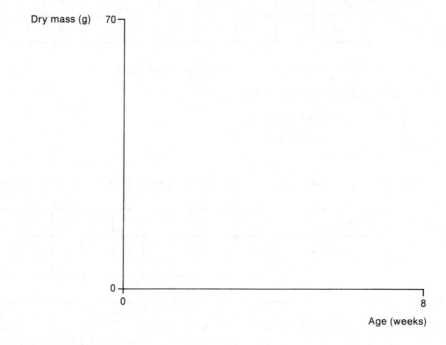

b) What is meant by 'dry mass'?

c) i) What happened to the dry mass of the seedlings during the first four
weeks?

ii) Why did the dry mass change during this time?

d) Use the graph to estimate the dry mass of twenty seedlings after eight weeks.

e) There is a rapid gain in dry mass during the final three weeks.

i) What process makes this rapid gain possible?

ii) Name *two* important substances used in this process.

f) i) How would you expect the results to differ if the experiment were carried out in the dark?

ii) How many seeds would then have to be sown in order to get the results of this experiment?

8 In a laboratory ten animals had just hatched in a cage. Their lengths were measured over a period of two weeks as they grew. The average lengths are given below.

Age (days)	1	2	3	5	6	8	9	10	12	13	14	16
Average length (mm)	3	3	5	5	8	8	8	12	12	12	17	17

a) Draw a growth curve from these results.

b) What do you think the animals in the cage were? Give a reason for your answer.

c) Explain why there is a sudden increase in length between days 2 and 3, 9 and 10, and 13 and 14.

d) Why is there no increase in length between days 6 and 9 and between days 10 and 13?

12 Cell Division

1 Choose words from this list to fill in the gaps in the passage below:

> 7 23 46 127 nucleus genes homologous
> divide number pairs staining

Chromosomes are found in the _____ of every living cell. They can be seen by _____ a cell that is about to _____ . For each thread-like chromosome there is another one exactly like it; therefore chromosomes occur in _____ . Every body cell of a particular organism has the same _____ of chromosomes. For example, all humans have _____ chromosomes in each body cell, made up of _____ pairs. The cells of the garden pea have 14 chromosomes made up of _____ pairs and those of the shrimp have 254 chromosomes, made up of _____ pairs. The two chromosomes belonging to a matching pair are called _____ chromosomes.

2   This is a drawing of the chromosomes of a fruit fly.

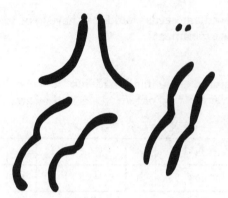

     a)   What is the chromosome number of this organism?

     b)   How many matching pairs are there?

3   The diagrams on the following page show stages in mitosis.

     a)   Using the identifying letters arrange these stages in the correct sequence.

     b)   Explain what is happening in each stage.

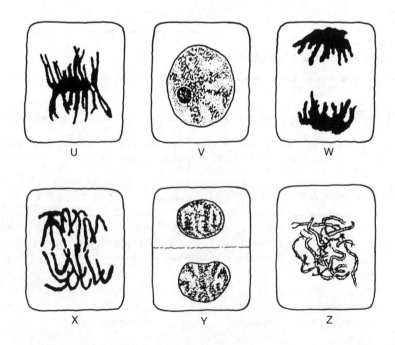

4   When organisms grow they increase the number of cells they are made of. A single cell divides to form two cells. The two new cells must have chromosomes that are identical to those of the original cell from which they were formed. In this way all the cells of an organism will have a set of chromosomes identical to that of the single fertilised egg from which they grew.

   a)   What name is given to the type of cell division that produces two cells that are identical to the parent cell?

   b)   Copy and complete the diagram below by drawing in the nuclei of the two cells produced when the original cell divides by **mitosis**.

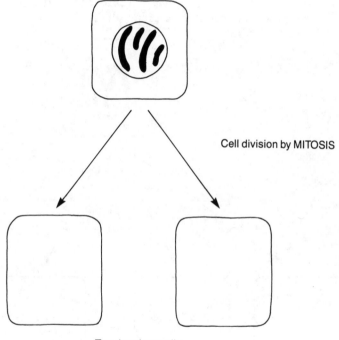

Cell division by MITOSIS

Two daughter cells

A cell of an imaginary organism with four chromosomes

5   a)   When would mitosis occur in *Amoeba*?

   b)   Where would you expect mitosis to occur in

      i)   a growing plant, such as a tree in spring?

      ii)   an adult human?

   c)   Complete this sentence:

            Cells divide by mitosis during _____ and _____ reproduction.

6 a) If a human egg and a human sperm each carried 46 chromosomes, how many chromosomes would there be in the fertilised egg?

b) How many chromosomes would there be in all the cells of the baby which grew from that fertilised egg?

c) How many chromosomes must there be in human eggs and sperms to prevent the doubling of the chromosome number?

7 **Meiosis** is the special process of cell division that occurs in the formation of gametes.

a) Copy and complete the diagram below by drawing in the nuclei of the four cells produced when the original cell divides by *meiosis*.

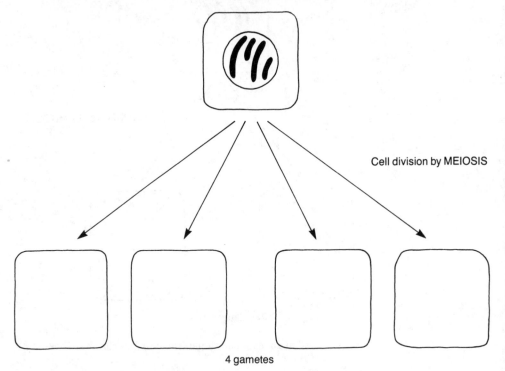

Cell division by MEIOSIS

4 gametes

b) Why is meiosis also known as 'reduction division'?

c) Where does meiosis occur in

i) a mammal?

ii) a flowering plant?

d) Explain why it is necessary for gametes to be formed in this way.

e) Copy and complete this sentence:

The nuclei of reproductive cells (gametes) contain only _____ member of each pair of _____ chromosomes.

8 In this diagram of the **human life cycle** the circles represent the cells:

a) Copy and complete the diagram below by writing in the circles the numbers of chromosomes found in those cells.

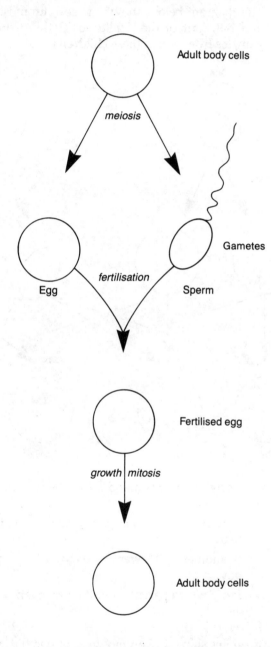

b) Which of the cells in the diagram are **diploid** (have the full number of chromosomes) and which are **haploid** (have only half the full number)?

9 a) What are **sex chromosomes**?

b) How do human males and females differ in their sex chromosomes?

c) How many sex chromosomes are found in a gamete?

d) The diagram below shows the sex chromosomes of a human couple, Ada and Bill, four of their children (Cathy, Dora, Edward and Fred) and the gametes from which these children began.

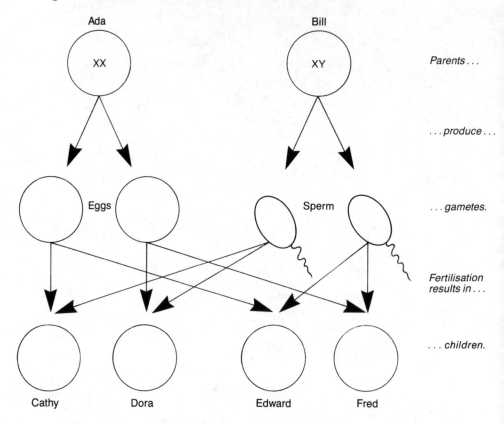

i)   Copy the diagram and fill in the sex chromosomes of the gametes and children.

ii) Is it the egg or the sperm nucleus which determines the sex of the baby?

iii) If another child was expected, what would be its chance of being a boy?

iv) From which parent would a boy inherit a Y chromosome?

10 The diagrams show the chromosomes of two different children.

a) Study the diagrams and give *two* differences between child A and child B.

b) Which child has an abnormal set of chromosomes?

c) What is the name of the genetic disorder caused by the abnormality?

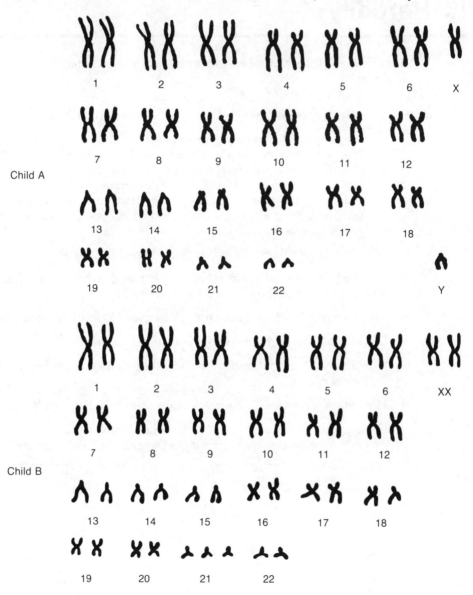

Child A

Child B

d) This abnormality can now be detected in an unborn baby by amniocentesis.

i) What does this process involve?

ii) What is the advantage of detecting such abnormalities in an unborn child?

e) What difference would you see if the chromosomes had been taken from a sex cell?

f) How can you tell that the body cell they came from was not a mature red blood cell?

13 Heredity

1 Use the word 'inheritance' in a sentence which shows that you understand its meaning.

2 Read the passage below and then answer the following questions.

> Gregor Mendel carried out experiments with pea plants. In one experiment he studied how the height of the pea plant was inherited. He took **pure-breeding** tall plants and crossed them with **pure-breeding** dwarf plants. He collected the pea seeds that were produced and grew them to produce the F_1 generation. All the F_1 plants were tall.
>
> He then allowed the F_1 tall plants to self-fertilise. He collected the seeds and grew them to produce the F_2 generation. Three-quarters of these plants were tall, and one-quarter were dwarf.

a) Who was Gregor Mendel? When and where did he live?

b) If pure-breeding tall plants are self-fertilised what kind of plants will always grow from the seeds that are produced?

c) Which characteristic is dominant, tall or dwarf? How do you know this?

d) Did Mendel know about genes when he did his work?

e) How many genes that control the height of the plants are found in each cell of the pea plants?

f) How many genes for height are found in a pollen grain nucleus or egg cell?

g) Let the gene for tallness $= T$; let the gene for dwarfism $= t$. Complete this diagram to show the genes present in the gametes and F_1 plants.

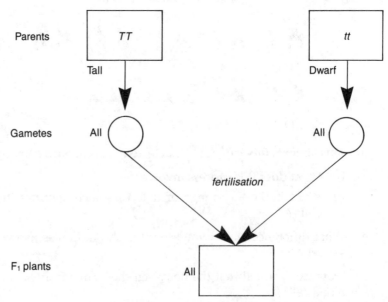

h) Copy this diagram, which shows the cross between the F_1 plants and complete it by writing in the boxes the genes of the parents and the F_2 plants.

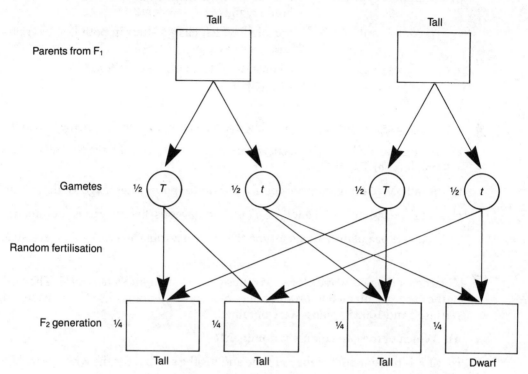

i) Why is a capital letter used to represent the gene for tallness and a small letter used for the gene for dwarfism?

3 Pea plants are normally self-pollinated. How did Mendel cross-pollinate the flowers in his experiments?

4 What are the *four* basic rules of **genetics** first discovered by Mendel?

5 Match the words in the left-hand column with the definitions in the right-hand column.

Words	Definitions
gene	having two identical genes for a particular characteristic
allele	an organism's outward appearance
phenotype	having two different genes for a particular characteristic
genotype	the genes that an organism contains

homozygous	a short length of DNA controlling an organism's characteristics
heterozygous	the allele which only has an effect when homozygous
dominant	the allele which has an effect in both homozygous and heterozygous conditions
recessive	a contrasting form of the gene for the same characteristic

6 Complete these sentences by choosing the correct word from inside the brackets:

a) A pea plant whose (genotype/phenotype) is tall, could have the (genotype/phenotype) *TT* or *Tt*.

b) A tall pea plant with genotype *TT* is (homozygous/heterozygous) dominant.

c) A tall pea plant with genotype *Tt* is (homozygous/heterozygous) dominant.

d) A dwarf pea plant with genotype *tt* is (homozygous/heterozygous) recessive.

7 A gardener crossed 50 red-flowered tulips with 50 white-flowered tulips. The seeds of the cross germinated to produce only red-flowered tulips (F_1). The F_1 were self-fertilised and 1000 F_2 plants were obtained.

a) Which of the two colours is dominant?

b) If R is the symbol for the red gene and r is the symbol for the white gene, how would you represent the F_1 plants?

c) Draw a diagram to explain how the F_2 generation plants were produced from the self-fertilising of the F_1 plants.

d) About how many red-flowered tulips would you expect in the F_2 generation?

e) About how many white-flowered tulips would you expect in the F_2 generation?

f) If a heterozygous red tulip (Rr) and a homozygous red tulip (RR) were each crossed with the recessive (white) parent, what differences would you expect to find between the two sets of offspring? Draw diagrams to show the crosses.

g) Give two reasons why plants are easier to use in genetic studies of this type than most animals?

8 In mice, the coat colour black is dominant over the coat colour brown. Let the gene for black coat $= B$ and the gene for brown coat $= b$.

a) Explain with the help of a diagram, how two black mice could produce a brown offspring.

b) If you had a black mouse, how could you prove that it was carrying a gene for brown coat colour, i.e. that it was heterozygous Bb?

9 In humans, the ability to roll the tongue is caused by a dominant gene. Using R to represent the gene for rolling and r that for non-rolling, explain the possible offspring that can be produced when the parents are:

a) a roller and a non-roller

b) two non-rollers

c) two rollers

10 a) How many alleles has the gene for ABO blood grouping in humans?

b) How many alleles for this are carried by each person?

c) Copy and complete this table.

Blood group (phenotype)	Possible genotypes
A B AB O	

d) The alleles A and B are co-dominant. What does this mean?

e) It is possible for all four blood groups to occur in the children of one family. Write a full genetic explanation of how this could happen.

f) A woman of blood group A claims that a man of blood group AB is the father of her child who is group O. Is this possible? Write out a full explanation of your answer.
Could he have been the father if he had been group B?

11 In Shorthorn cattle the alleles for coat colour are co-dominant. If a red cow is crossed with a white bull the calves all have a mixture of red and white hairs and are called **roans**. (The same happens with a white cow and a red bull.)

What are the possible coat colours in the offspring produced from crossing a roan cow and a roan bull? Write out a full explanation of your answer.

12 Choose words from the list below to complete the following sentences. Each word can be used once, more than once or not at all.

> allele   cells   chromosome   dominant   gametes   gene
> harmful   mutant   mutation   one   recessive   two
> random

a) A change in a gene or a chromosome is called a _____.

b) Mutations occur naturally at _____.

c) Most mutations are _____.

d) Mutation can result in the formation of a new _____ for a particular characteristic.

e) In order to be passed on to the next generation, mutations must occur in cells from which _____ are formed, or in the _____ themselves.

f) Down's syndrome is caused by a _____ mutation. People with Down's syndrome have _____ extra _____.

g) Most mutations produce _____ alleles and only show up if identical mutant alleles happen to occur in the same person.

h) Albinism is caused by a mutation in the _____ for the production of skin pigments.

13 Mutations occur constantly in populations. However it is possible to increase the rate at which mutations occur.

List *four* agents which can cause mutations.

14 Opposite is a diagram of part of the family tree of Queen Victoria. (Not all of her children are shown.) It shows how the disease **haemophilia** occurred in some of her descendants. Haemophilia had not occurred in any of the ancestors of Queen Victoria or Prince Albert.

The gene causing haemophilia is carried on the X chromosome.

a) If X = normal chromosome, X^h = chromosome carrying the haemophilia gene, a normal male has genotype XY, and a normal female has genotype XX, what are the genotypes of

   i)   a haemophiliac male?

   ii) a haemophiliac female?

   iii) a female who appears normal but carries the gene for haemophilia?

   Use the information in the family tree to answer the following questions:

b) Is the gene that causes haemophilia recessive or dominant with respect to the normal gene? Explain your answer.

c) From which parent did Prince Leopold inherit the haemophilia gene? Explain your choice.

d) Copy the family tree. Shade the females who are shown to be carriers as ◗.

e) Use the symbols X, X^h and Y to explain how haemophilia was passed down from Leopold to his grandson.

f) If haemophilia did not occur in any of the ancestors of either Queen Victoria or Prince Albert, how do you account for its appearance in their children?

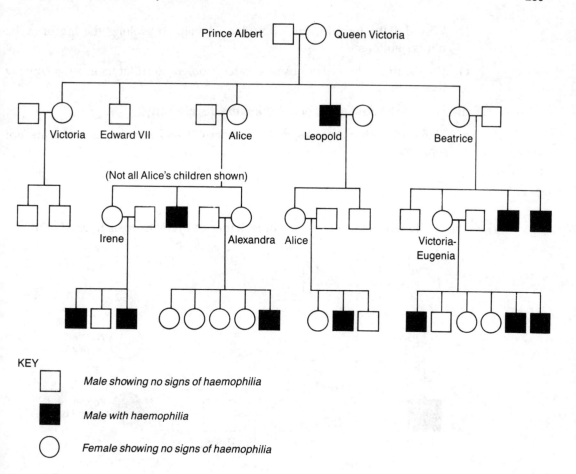

KEY

◻ *Male showing no signs of haemophilia*

◼ *Male with haemophilia*

◯ *Female showing no signs of haemophilia*

15 Read this passage which is about **cystic fibrosis** and then answer the following questions.

> Cystic fibrosis is an inherited disease caused by a recessive allele which is a mutant form of the normal allele found in healthy people. Children with this disease produce very sticky mucus which clogs the lungs and intestines. This leads to infection and serious tissue damage. Before the introduction of antibiotics most sufferers died in infancy due to constant infections. Drugs are now available which are inhaled as a vapour and soften the mucus helping to prevent infection. Cystic fibrosis also makes sweat more salty. Simple tests on sweat can help to detect the disease in infancy and allow doctors to start treatment before irreversible lung damage has been done.

a) Explain the meaning of the following as used in the first sentence of the passage:

i)   an inherited disease

ii)   a recessive allele

iii) a mutant form of the normal allele

b) Why did the introduction of antibiotics help to prolong the life of cystic fibrosis sufferers?

c) Why would salty sweat pose a greater problem to sufferers in a hot country than in Britain?

d) What is the advantage of detecting the disease early?

e) Name *two* other diseases that are inherited and *two* diseases that are not inherited.

16 The family tree below shows the **inheritance of cystic fibrosis** in one family.

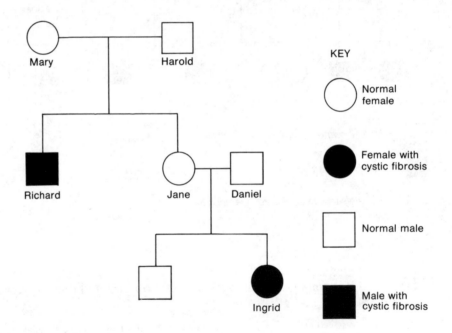

a) Select symbols to represent the normal and cystic fibrosis alleles.

b) Give the **genotypes** of each of the people named in the family.

c) What are the possible genotypes of the son of Jane and Daniel?

d) If Jane and Daniel have another child what is the probability of its being

   i)   completely normal

   ii)   a sufferer from cystic fibrosis

   iii) a carrier of the disease?

e) After the discovery that Ingrid had cystic fibrosis, Jane and Daniel went to see a genetic counsellor. What would have been the purpose of such a visit?

17 **Huntington's chorea** is a terrible neuropsychiatric disorder. It can start at any age but most commonly in the 40s and 50s. Patients suffer personality changes and a decreasing ability to control their movements. Everyday actions such as walking, using cutlery and speech become increasingly difficult, or even impossible. Dementia affects most if not all patients as the disease progresses. The symptoms get relentlessly worse leading inevitably to death within 15 years. There is no cure.

The disease is inherited and is dominant. It occurs in individuals with only a single dose of the abnormal gene; affected individuals are therefore said to be **heterozygous**.

The diagram below shows a typical pedigree for Huntington's chorea.

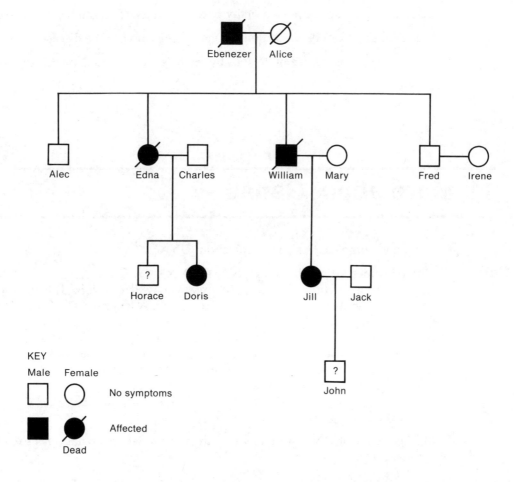

a) Select symbols to represent the normal and Huntington's chorea alleles.

b) Give the genotypes of each of the people named in the family except for John and Horace.

c) What are John and Horace's possible genotypes?

d) What proportion of an affected person's gametes would carry the disease gene?

e) Fred, aged 28, the youngest son of Ebenezer and Alice, has just married Irene.

   If you were a genetic counsellor what advice would you give them about starting a family? What are the risks they face?

18 Identify the three inherited diseases described below from the choice given:

   Huntington's chorea   cystic fibrosis   haemophilia

   _____ can be passed on by parents neither of whom has the disease.

   _____ can be passed on by one parent who has the disease.

   _____ is passed on to sons by females who do not have the disease.

14 More about Genes

1 Copy and complete this paragraph about **DNA**.

Chromosomes are made up of DNA. DNA is short for _____. It carries the coded instructions for how an organism will develop. The instructions control the synthesis of _____ in the cell. A length of DNA which codes for one protein is called a _____. Most of the proteins produced by a cell are _____. The DNA molecule is made up of two strands twisted together into a spiral or double _____. Untwisted the molecule is like a _____ whose rungs are made up of pairs of organic _____. There are _____ different bases.

2 a) The bases of DNA are known by their initial letters. What does each letter stand for?

   i)   A =

   ii) C =

   iii) T =

   iv) G =

b)   The diagram below shows a small part of a DNA molecule. The bases are labelled only on one strand. Copy the diagram and label all the bases.

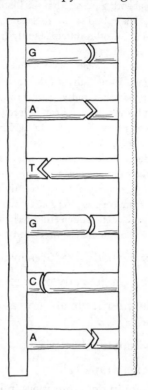

3   Copy and complete these sentences.

a)   A protein is a long chain of _____ in a specific sequence. There are _____ different amino acids.

b)   A _____ is a row of three bases on a DNA strand. It codes for one _____.

c)   Protein synthesis occurs in structures in the cytoplasm called _____.

d)   A molecule called _____ RNA is a copy of a portion of _____. It carries genetic information from the nucleus to the _____.

e)   The order of _____ in the m RNA controls the order of _____ in a protein molecule.

4   Read this passage which is about **genetic engineering** and then answer the following questions:

> Genetic engineering uses techniques that allow scientists to transfer genes from one organism to another. Simple, rapidly reproducing organisms like bacteria can be used as chemical factories for making substances needed by other organisms, such as humans. An example is insulin.

Many people suffer from a disease called diabetes, which means that they cannot make the hormone insulin. In healthy people it is produced after a meal and instructs the tissues to absorb glucose from the blood. Many diabetics inject insulin, taken from animals, into their bodies to replace the insulin they cannot make themselves. However, animal insulin differs slightly from the human variety and sometimes has unpleasant side effects.

Scientists now use genetic engineering to produce human insulin. They can transfer the insulin gene from human cells to a bacterium by using special enzymes. The bacterium reproduces rapidly, soon producing millions of bacterial cells, all able to make human insulin. Bacteria can be grown in huge numbers in large vats like those used for brewing beer. Therefore in the future the use of human insulin produced by bacteria should be common.

Another disease that some people have stops them from producing growth hormone in their pituitary glands. Unfortunately only human growth hormone can be used to treat these people. Until recently this could only be obtained from pituitary glands taken from corpses. Very large numbers of pituitary glands are needed to treat one individual. Genetic engineering techniques have now been developed that enable human growth hormone to be produced by bacteria.

a) Which organ of the body produces insulin?

b) What is the effect on the body of a deficiency of insulin?

c) Why is insulin from animals not as desirable for treating diabetics as human insulin?

d) Why is it significant that bacteria

  i) reproduce very rapidly?

  ii) can be grown in huge numbers in large vats?

e) What is the effect on the body of a deficiency of growth hormone?

f) Explain how genetic engineering could be used to produce human growth hormone.

5 Biologists have managed to change the genes in larger animals like mice. the diagram opposite shows how giant mice have been bred by genetic engineering. Study the diagram and answer the questions below.

a) How would the mice eggs have been fertilised?

b) What are plasmids?

c) Which human gene has been inserted into the plasmids?

d) What caused some of the baby mice to grow up to 25% bigger than their parents?

e) Would you expect the offspring of these giant mice to be normal or giant? Explain why.

f) Should biologists be allowed to carry out this kind of experiment? What are the possible consequences of such research?

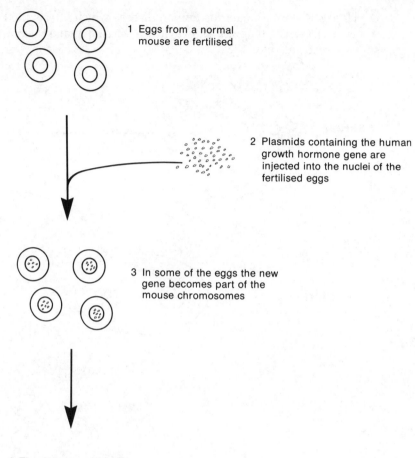

1 Eggs from a normal mouse are fertilised

2 Plasmids containing the human growth hormone gene are injected into the nuclei of the fertilised eggs

3 In some of the eggs the new gene becomes part of the mouse chromosomes

4 The eggs are put back into a female mouse and allowed to develop

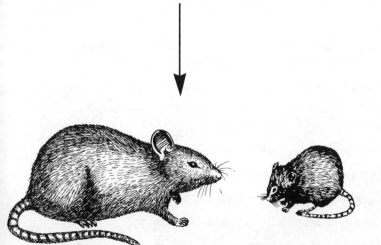

5 Some of the mice produced from these eggs grow to be giant mice

6 Hepatitis B is a dangerous human disease which affects the liver and is caused by a virus. The diagram shows how a vaccine against hepatitis B can be made by genetic engineering.

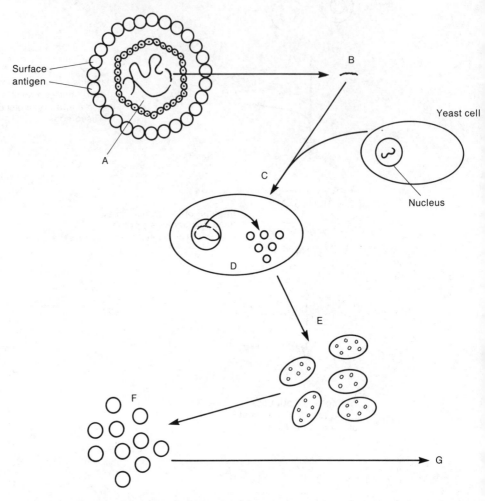

a) Copy the diagram and then annotate it by correctly matching each stage labelled A–G with the statement given below.

The genetically engineered yeast cell responds by producing surface antigen protein.

Basis for the vaccine against hepatitis B

Large numbers of yeast cells are cultured.

Hepatitis B virus with surface antigen gene in its DNA

Surface antigen protein is extracted and purified.

Surface antigen gene is cut out of DNA by an enzyme.

Surface antigen gene is inserted into yeast DNA by another enzyme.

b) What is an antigen?

c) How will the body respond when this vaccine enters the blood stream?

d) How will this reaction protect the body against hepatitis B?

e) Some vaccines are made from weak doses of the microbe. Why is the above process so much safer and more effective in the case of hepatitis B.

15 Variation

1 Complete these sentences by choosing the correct word from inside the brackets:

a) Offspring produced by asexual reproduction are always (different/identical) and so there is (no/much) variation.

b) Offspring produced by sexual reproduction are always (different/identical) and so there is (no/much) variation.

2 a) This bar chart illustrates an example of **continuous variation**. Between the tallest and the shortest oak tree there is a complete range of intermediates.

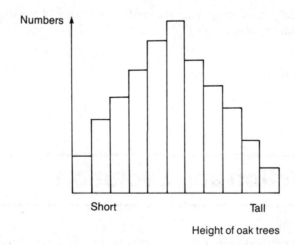

i) Copy the bar chart.

ii) List *three* examples of continuous variation in humans.

b) This bar chart illustrates an example of **discontinuous variation**. The pea plants are either tall or dwarf. There are no 'in-betweens'.

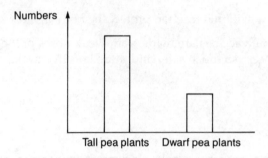

i)   Copy the bar chart.

ii) List *three* examples of discontinuous variation in humans.

c) Explain the difference between continuous and discontinuous variation.

3 a) i)   List *three* ways in which all humans are alike.

ii) List *three* ways in which humans differ from one another.

b) Variation occurs in many other species of animals and plants, for example:

> **number of petals on a daisy flower**
> **colour of tulip flowers**
> **height of oak trees**
> **coat colour of labrador dogs.**

Make a list of at least *six* further examples of variation found in animal and plant species.

4 List *three* causes of variation.

16 Selection and Evolution

1 a) What were the earliest forms of life on Earth, small simple organisms or large complex ones?

b) Where were the earliest forms of life to be found?

c) What is meant by evolution?

d)   Try to find out how many millions of years ago scientists believe that

    i)   the Earth was formed

    ii)   the first life evolved

    iii)   the dinosaurs died out

    iv)   modern Man (*Homo sapiens*) appeared

2   Read this passage about fossils from *Life on Earth* by David Attenborough and then answer the questions which follow:

> The vast majority of animals leave no trace of their existence after their passing. Their flesh decays, their shells and their bones become scattered and turn to powder. But very occasionally, one or two individuals out of a population of many thousands have a different fate. A reptile becomes stuck in a swamp and dies. Its body rots but its bones settle into the mud. Dead vegetation drifts to the bottom and covers them. As the centuries pass and more vegetation accumulates, the deposit turns to peat. Changes in sea level may cause the swamp to be flooded and layers of sand to be deposited on top of the peat. Over great periods of time, the peat is compressed and turned to coal. The reptile's bones still remain within it. The great pressure of the overlying sediments and the mineral-rich solutions that circulate through them cause chemical changes in the calcium phosphate of the bones. Eventually they are turned to stone, but they retain not only the outward shape that they had in life, albeit sometimes distorted, but on occasion even their detailed cellular structure is preserved so that you can look at sections of them through the microscope and plot the shape of the blood vessels and the nerves that once surrounded them.
>
> The most suitable places for fossilisation are in seas and lakes where sedimentary deposits like sandstones and limestones are slowly accumulating. On land, where for the most part rocks are not built up by deposition but broken down by erosion, deposits, such as sand dunes, are only very rarely created and preserved. In consequence, the only land-living creatures likely to be fossilised are those that happen to fall into water.

a)   Explain why 'the vast majority of animals leave no trace of their existence after their passing'.

b)   What is a fossil?

c)   In what type of rocks can fossils be found?

d)   Why are the hard parts of animals such as shells and bones more likely to be preserved?

e)   Why are water living organisms more often fossilised than land living organisms?

f)   Briefly   describe two other ways in which organisms may be naturally preserved.

g)   What evidence is there from fossils to suggest that reptiles lived before mammals?

3 All vertebrates possess the same pattern of bones in their limbs. This suggests that
they have all evolved from a common ancestor.

a) What are vertebrates?

b) What is meant by a 'common ancestor'?

c) Label the diagram of the pentadactyl limb pattern with the names of the bones
of the front and hind limbs of mammals (e.g. humans).

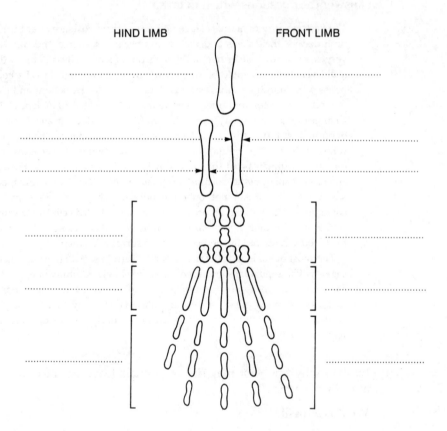

d) The following diagrams show how this basic limb structure has become
adapted for different purposes. Decide which limb belongs to each of these
animals:

    bat
    bird
    horse
    human
    whale

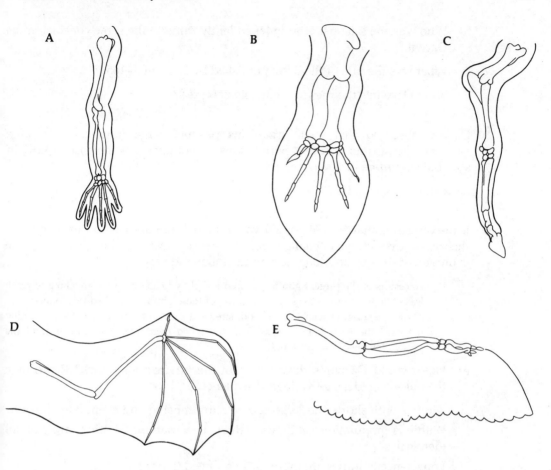

4 Today, most scientists accept the theories of evolution first put forward by Charles Darwin in 1858. Use reference books to find out about Darwin and answer the following questions:

a) Before the 19th century, how did people believe that new species came about? (Some people still believe this today.)

b) When was Darwin born?

c) What was the name of the ship on which he sailed to South America in 1832?

d) How long did the voyage last?

e) Which islands did Darwin visit and where are they?

f) What did he find particularly interesting about the wildlife on these islands?

g) How long after his return to England did Darwin publish his theory? Why do you think it took him so long?

h)   Who was the scientist who independently came to the same conclusions as Darwin?

i)   What was the title of the book published by Darwin in 1859?

j)   Were Darwin's theories immediately accepted?

5 Darwin observed that most organisms produce large numbers of young. However, he also noticed that populations do not generally increase rapidly in size, but stay more or less constant.

How did he explain this?

6 Jean-Baptiste Lamarck (1744–1829) was a French biologist who put forward a theory of evolutionary change before that of Darwin. He explained the evolution of the giraffe's long neck in the following way:

> Ancestors of the present giraffe acquired a slightly longer neck by stretching to reach leaves high up in the trees. The offspring of these giraffes inherited this longer neck. These offspring, in reaching for food, stretched their necks more and their offspring inherited the even longer necks. This continued over many generations until the present long neck was acquired.

a)   How would Darwin's theory explain the giraffe's long neck? Re-arrange the following ideas into a logical sequence:

Giraffes with shorter necks would be outnumbered and eventually die out.

Within a population of giraffes there is variation, i.e. they are not all identical.

Longer-neck giraffes are more likely to breed/rear offspring.

Giraffes with longer necks could reach food at a greater height unavailable to others.

Offspring would inherit the characteristic for a longer neck.

Some giraffes carry genes for a longer neck.

Giraffes with longer necks could see predators at greater distances.

Longer-neck giraffes are more likely to survive to maturity.

b)   Explain how natural selection has been involved in *one* of the following situations:

i)   The peppered moth exists in two forms, pale and dark. In industrial areas the dark variety is the commoner. In country areas the pale variety is the commoner.

ii)   There are some bacteria that were once killed by penicillin, but are now resistant to it.

iii) New types of mosquito have arisen which are resistant to DDT.

iv)   Rats are normally killed by a poison called warfarin, but the number of rats that are not affected by the poison is on the increase.

7 The peppered moth lives in woods, feeding at night and resting on the lichen covered bark of trees during the daytime. The moth is usually speckled black and white, but some are so heavily speckled that they appear almost black. The moths are eaten by robins, thrushes and fly-catchers in the daytime.

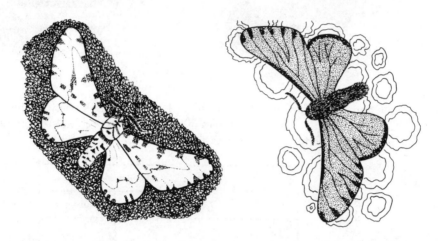

An investigation was carried out in which peppered moths were released in two different areas, and then some time later recaptured and counted. The results are shown in the table below. Study the results and then answer the questions.

	Dorset *(agricultural area)*		Birmingham *(industrial area)*	
	Speckled	*Black*	*Speckled*	*Black*
Number released	496	473	137	447
Number recaptured	62	30	18	123
Percentage recaptured	12.5	6.3	13.0	27.5

a) Which type of moth survived best in Dorset? Suggest a reason why.

b) Which type of moth survived best in Birmingham? Suggest a reason why.

c) What effect might the Clean Air Act have on future populations of the peppered moth in industrial areas?

d) The gene for the dark form of the peppered moth is dominant to the gene for the light form. Suggest with reasons how this will affect:

   i) the survival of the gene for the light form of peppered moth in a population in an industrial area.

   ii) the survival of the gene for the dark form of the peppered moth in a population in a rural area.

8
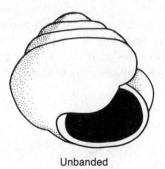
Unbanded

Banded

The above are drawings of a banded and an unbanded variety of the snail species *Cepaea nemoralis*. Random samples of these snails were collected from two different sites and the numbers recorded as shown in the following table.

Site	Number of snails	
	Banded	Unbanded
Grassland	29	70
Under hedgerows	89	10

a)   How might random samples have been collected?

b)   Suggest two hypotheses to account for the relative abundance of banded snails under hedgerows.

c)   Design a simple experiment to test one of your hypotheses.

9 a)   How is the breeding of dogs

i)   similar to

ii) different from

the process of evolution by natural selection?

b)   What are the advantages to man of breeding new varieties of food crops such as wheat, maize and rice by artificial selection?

10 Read the following passage about **selective breeding**, and answer the questions.

Man has cultivated plants and kept animals for about 10 000 years. Over this time he has bred them selectively to produce desirable characteristics. For example, modern varieties of cattle have been bred over a very long time to give a high milk yield or fast meat production. From the varied individuals amongst a herd of cattle, breeders choose only those with desirable characteristics to breed and produce the next generation. Plant breeders have bred varieties of wheat and rice that grow more quickly, give a higher yield of grain and are more resistant to disease.

However the varieties of animals and plants that have been specially bred by man, would very often be unable to survive in the wild. Some farmers are now beginning to think differently about the characteristics they want in their animals and plants. Instead of enormous yields, they are now looking for varieties of crops that can grow well with less fertilisers or pesticides and varieties of animals that require less expensive housing and food. Luckily many of the older breeds that have these desirable characteristics have been conserved. These can be used in breeding programmes to develop new varieties.

a) What is meant by 'selective breeding'?

b) What are the advantages to man of breeding new varieties of food crops, such as wheat and rice?

c) According to the passage, what characteristics might be developed by plant and animal breeders in the future?

d) Why is it important to conserve the older varieties of animals and plants?

11 Read this passage and answer the questions that follow it. The passage is about the **evolution of bread wheat** and is adapted from *The Ascent of Man* by J. Bronowksi

The turning point in the spread of agriculture was almost certainly the occurrence of two forms of wheat with large, full heads of seeds. Before 8 000 BC, wheat was not the luxuriant plant it is today; it was merely one of many wild grasses that spread throughout the Middle East. By some genetic accident, the wild wheat crossed with a natural goat grass and formed a fertile hybrid. The fourteen chromosomes of wild wheat were combined with the fourteen chromosomes of goat grass, and produced **Emmer** with twenty-eight chromosomes. The seeds of Emmer wheat were much plumper than the wild wheat and were attached to the husk in such a way that they scattered in the wind. For such a hybrid to be fertile is rare but not unique among plants.

There was a second genetic accident in which Emmer crossed with another natural goat grass and produced a still larger hybrid with forty-two chromosomes, which is **bread wheat**. However this wheat can only be propagated by man. The seeds will never spread in the wind because the ear is too tight to break up. The life of each, man and plant, depends on the other. It is a true fairy tale of genetics — as if the coming of civilisation had been blessed in advance by the spirit of the abbot Gregor Mendel.

a) Why was the occurrence of wheat with large full heads of seeds a 'turning point' to the spread of agriculture?

b) Consider a plant with a chromosome number of fourteen.

i) How many chromosomes would you normally expect to find in the gametes of this plant?

ii) What would you expect to be the chromosome number of the offspring grown from a seed of this plant?

c) Why is the crossing of wild wheat with a natural goat grass described as a genetic accident?

d) What is a 'hybrid'?

e) Why would bread wheat not survive in the wild?

Theme 6

How Organisms Affect Humans

1 Organisms as Food for Humans

1 Make a list of

   a) *ten* plants

   b) *five* animals

   that humans use as food.

2 Choose one of the organisms you named in Question 1 and find out more about

   a) the organism itself

   b) how it is cultivated or reared

3 Read this passage which is about micro-organisms as food for humans and answer
the following questions.

> Bacteria can be grown to make a protein-rich food called single-cell protein (SCP).
> A variety of substances can be used by the bacteria to produce SCP. These include
> natural gas, methanol, manure and food wastes such as citrus peel and milk whey.
> SCP is an excellent protein which can be produced quickly, in vast quantities. Its
> production uses little space and it can be easily stored as a powder. It is used at
> present as an animal feed for chickens and calves, but could be used for human
> consumption.
>
> Mycoprotein is a fungus. It contains about 45 per cent protein and is high in fibre.
> It can be used to make artificial meat by adding appropriate flavourings. It has a
> texture which is chewy and similar to meat.

   a) What organisms are used to make SCP?

   b) Name one food waste used as a food base for SCP production.

   c) Give *three* advantages of SCP.

   d) Why do you think it is used only as animal food at the moment?

   e) What is mycoprotein?

   f) Why is mycoprotein more suitable than SCP for human consumption?

4 Study the bar chart which compares the nutrients in mycoprotein and in beef, and
answer the following questions.

   a) Give three reasons why mycoprotein is a healthier food than beef. Explain your
reasons.

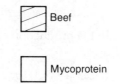

Beef

Mycoprotein

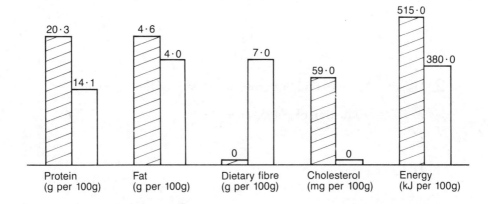

					515·0
20·3		4·6		7·0	
			4·0		380·0
	14·1			59·0	
		0		0	
Protein	Fat	Dietary fibre	Cholesterol	Energy
(g per 100g)	(g per 100g)	(g per 100g)	(mg per 100g)	(kJ per 100g)

b) Give two reasons why it would be better to eat beef than mycoprotein.

c) Some people find mycoprotein unpleasant to eat and it goes bad quickly. Suggest two types of food additive which could help to overcome these problems. Give an example of each type.

2 Useful Microbes

1 Choose words from this list to complete the following sentences:

milk   bread   penicillin   microbes   antibiotics   yeast
decay   protein   bacteria   vinegar   biotechnology

a) The use of microbes in industrial processes is known as _____.

b) Bacteria and fungi play a very important part in making dead organisms
_____.

c) The process of sewage treatment depends on decay _____.

d) Butter, yoghurt, and cheese are made by the action of bacteria on _____.

e) The flavour of different cheeses is due to the action of different _____.

f) _____ is used to produce alcohol and to make _____ rise.

g) In the production of _____, bacteria are used to convert ethanol to acetic acid.

h) Bacteria and fungi can now be grown in special chambers to produce _____ as food for humans and animals.

i) Some microbes produce substances that can kill other microbes and prevent them from multiplying. These substances are called _____. An example of one is _____.

2 Use the library to find out more about each of the following:

a) The production of butter, cheese and yoghurt

b) Brewing

c) Bread-making

3 The diagrams below show the results of an experiment using yeast and sugar solutions carried out at a temperature of 20 °C.

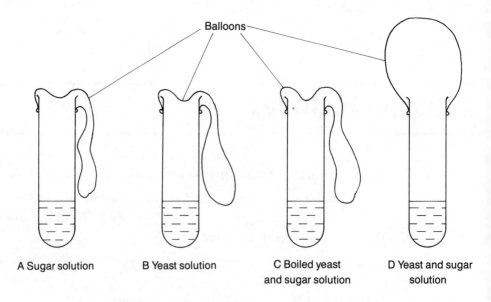

A Sugar solution   B Yeast solution   C Boiled yeast and sugar solution   D Yeast and sugar solution

a) Explain why the balloon has blown up in Tube D.

b) Explain why the balloons have not blown up in Tubes A, B and C.

c) Name *two* substances that would be produced in the test-tube containing yeast and sugar solution?

d) What would have been the result if dry yeast and sugar had been used instead of solutions? Explain your answer.

e) What would you expect the results to be if the yeast and sugar solution had been kept at the following temperatures?

    i)   0 °C

    ii)   35 °C

    iii) 80 °C

4

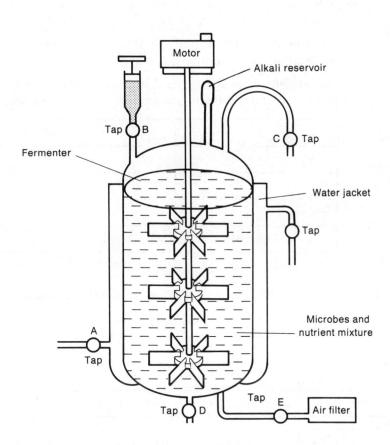

The diagram above shows an **industrial fermenter**. These are large containers in which microbes such as penicillin can be grown. There are many pipes and the taps are used to control the entry and exit of different substances.

a) Copy the above diagram.

b) Match the taps labelled A–E in the left-hand column with their correct functions in the right-hand column.

Taps *Function*
A   adding nutrients and/or culture organisms to the mixture
B   adding air to the mixture
C   allowing waste gases to escape
D   draining off the products
E   pumping cold water into the water jacket

c) What is the function of
   i)   the motor?
   ii) the air filter?

d) Why is cold water needed in the water jacket?

e) When empty, the fermenter is pumped through with steam. What is the reason for this?

f) Fermentation would stop if the pH of the mixture dropped. Describe how an optimum pH would be maintained.

g) The fermenter can also be used to produce mycoprotein. To do so, certain substances and conditions are needed. Copy and complete this table.

Substance or condition needed	Reason
Oxygen	
Sugar	
Ammonia	
Constant temperature of 32°C	

5 a) Copy the diagram, which represents a **sewage works**.

b) Copy and complete the following table:

Part of sewage works	Description of the process that occurs there
A Sieve	
B Grit tank	Heavy particles such as grit sink to the bottom and can be removed.
C Settlement tank	
D Filter bed	
E Humus tank	The liquid leaving the filter beds contains dead plants and animals which lived among the stones in the filter bed. This is *humus*. In the humus tank the liquid is left undisturbed so that the humus settles to the bottom and the purified effluent can be separated and passed into a river.

c)   Use the information in the table to label the parts A to E on your diagrams.

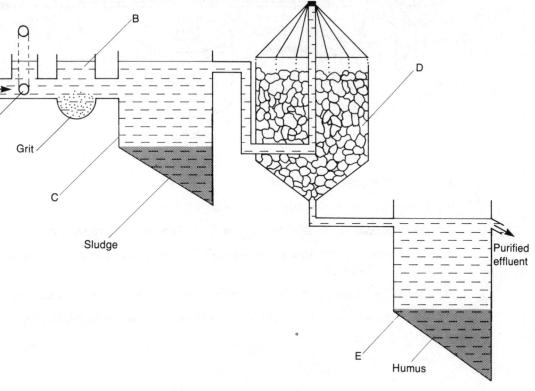

Grit

B

Sludge

C

D

Purified
effluent

E

Humus

d)   What is sewage? Why is it dangerous to health?

e)   How is the sewage carried to the sewage works?

f)   Anaerobic bacteria feed on the sludge and produce a gas which can be used as
a fuel to run the sewage works. When this process is complete, the sludge is
dried.

i)   Name the gas produced.

ii)   What can the dried sludge be used for?

g)   What other methods are used for the disposal of sewage?

6   Read this short passage about the production of biogas, then answer the following
questions.

> When vegetable and animal matter rots in the absence of air, a gas is given off. The
> gas is usually about 60 per cent methane, the rest being mostly carbon dioxide. This
> biogas is a good fuel, particularly for cooking, heating and lighting in the home.
>   Rubbish is often tipped into holes in the ground. This is called landfill. This
> rubbish will also generate biogas.

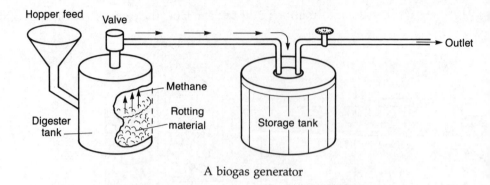

A biogas generator

a)   Why is the gas called biogas?

b)   Why is biogas particularly easy to make on farms?

c)   What use can be made of the solid material left behind in the digestor?

d)   What type of organisms are responsible for producing biogas from vegetable and animal matter?

e)   Design and draw a suitable method for collecting biogas from a landfill site.

f)   What kinds of household rubbish would work best at producing biogas?

3 Food Spoilage and its Prevention

1 What causes food to go bad?

2 Write down *two* reasons why it is necessary to preserve food. (Do not give the reason 'because it stops it from going bad'.)

3 Food may be preserved in the following ways: bottling, canning, drying, deep freezing, pasteurising, pickling, smoking, vacuum packing, ultra heat treating, irradiation.

a)   Copy the table opposite and fill in the spaces.

b)   Which of the methods in part a) above
    i)   kill the bacteria?
    ii)   only slow down the growth of the bacteria?

Name of method of food preservation	Description of the method
	Heat to 70 °C for fifteen seconds, then cool rapidly.
Pickling	
Bottling	
	Heat to drive out the air and kill bacteria, then seal the container.
	Draw air out of a polythene bag and then seal it.
Smoking	
Freezing	
	Heat to remove water.
Ultra heat treating	
Irradiation	

4 Suggest reasons for each of the following:

a)   Food kept in a refrigerator will eventually go bad.

b)   Frozen food should be eaten as soon as possible after it is taken out of the freezer.

c)   Dehydrated foods are often air-lifted to famine areas.

d)   Ultra heat treated milk is known as 'long life' milk.

e)   Pasteurised milk will turn sour quickly if it is not kept in a refrigerator.

f)   Salt meat used to be taken on long sea voyages.

g)   Meat should not be kept lukewarm (20–40 °C) for long periods.

h)   Frozen chickens should be completely defrosted before cooking.

i)   Biscuits will keep for long periods without going mouldy, but bread will not.

j)   When ultra heat treated milk has been opened it must be kept in a refrigerator.

5 Look at *ten* foods kept in your home. Record information about them in a table with these headings:

Name of food	How is it preserved?	Approximately how long will it keep?

4 Microbes and Disease

1 Name a disease

a) which is infectious

b) which is inherited

c) which is caused by a poor diet

d) which is caused by harmful chemicals

e) whose cause is unknown

f) which is transmitted only by sexual intercourse

2 Choose one disease caused by each of the following organisms:

a bacterium   a virus   a fungus   a protist

Record information about each disease by filling in the spaces in the following table:

Name of disease	Caused by	Main symptoms	Spread by
	a bacterium		
	a virus		
	a fungus		
	a protist		

3 Write a short account of how

a) the skin

b) the nasal and bronchial passages

c) the stomach

d) platelets

e) the phagocytes (white blood cells)

f) the lymphocytes (white blood cells)

help to protect us against harmful microbes.

4 a)   Use the library to find out about the life of **Louis Pasteur**.

  b)   Read the following passage carefully and then answer the questions.

> In 1866 Louis Pasteur was asked to investigate a mysterious disease that was
> killing off silk-worms in France and bringing ruin to farmers.
>   Pasteur already knew about microbes and he suspected that they might be the
> cause of the disease. So he carried our the following experiment. He took a healthy
> silk-moth, killed it and crushed up the body. He looked at it under a microscope
> and could see only the cells of the moth. He then took a diseased moth, crushed it
> and looked at it under the microscope. He saw bacteria mixed with the cells of the
> moth.

  i)   Why was it important for the silk farmers to find the cause of the disease?

  ii)   Why did they ask Louis Pasteur to help them?

  iii) What did Pasteur suspect was the cause of the disease?

  iv)   What difference did Pasteur find between the healthy and the diseased
         moths?

  v)   Did Pasteur prove that the bacteria were the cause of the disease? If not,
         what further experiments might he have done?

5 Diseases may be spread by such things as droplets in the air, dust, touch, faeces,
animals, cuts and scratches. Copy this table and fill in the blank spaces.

Description of the way in which a disease may be spread	An example of a disease spread in this way
By touching an infected person, or something that the infected person has touched	
	viral hepatitis
By being bitten by an animal carrying the disease	
	cholera
	smallpox
By breathing in water droplets containing germs, which have been breathed, coughed or sneezed out by an infected person	

6 Read this passage and then answer the following questions about Jenner's discovery of vaccination.

> Edward Jenner first used vaccination at the end of the eighteenth century. Girls who milked cows caught a mild disease called cowpox. After they had had cowpox, they did not seem to catch smallpox. Jenner carried out an experiment. He obtained some pus from a scab on the hand of a dairymaid with cowpox. He then scratched some of the pus into the arm of an eight-year-old boy called James Phipps. The boy caught cowpox but soon recovered. Jenner then transferred pus from a smallpox victim to James. James did not catch smallpox.

a) What observation led Jenner to make his discovery?

b) Describe the experiment Jenner carried out.

c) What would most likely have happened to James Phipps if Jenner's experiment had not worked? What would have happened to Jenner in that case?

d) Why was Jenner's discovery so important?

e) Jenner called his method of protecting people against smallpox 'vaccination'. Choose two words from this list which are often used nowadays instead of 'vaccination':

   infusion   inoculation   injection   immunisation

f) Why are people no longer vaccinated against smallpox?

7 Read this passage and then answer the questions below:

> In 1881 a French scientist made a vaccine against a bacterial disease called anthrax. His vaccine was made from weakened anthrax bacteria, produced by keeping them at 42–43 °C for a week.
>   In his experiment, he injected 30 sheep with a weak dose of the vaccine. Two weeks later he injected a second stronger dose of vaccine. Two weeks later he injected a strong dose of anthrax bacteria. The sheep did not develop anthrax. A second group of 30 sheep which had not been vaccinated were given the strong dose of bacteria at the same time. These sheep died.

a) What was the name of the scientist?

b) Why did the vaccine contain weakened anthrax bacteria?

c) Why should keeping the bacteria at 42–43 °C for a week weaken them?

d) Why were *two* doses of vaccine given?

e) Explain carefully why the vaccinated sheep survived but the others did not.

f) An extra group of sheep were included in the experiment. They were kept in the same field but neither vaccinated nor injected with anthrax bacteria. What was the reason for this?

g) In what way was the French scientist's experiment on anthrax a better scientific investigation than Jenner's experiment?

8 a) If a person is 'immune' to a disease what does this mean?

   b) Explain two ways in which it is possible to become immune to measles.

   c) Here is a brief outline of immunisation. Use it to write a complete paragraph
       called 'How immunisation works'.

   > **A small weak dose of microbes is injected or given by mouth.**
   > **Microbes multiply inside the body.**
   > **Antibodies are made.**
   > **Microbes are destroyed by the antibodies.**
   > **Antibodies remain in the blood.**
   > **Booster doses of vaccine are given. More antibodies are made.**
   > **Antibodies protect against the disease for several years.**

   d) i) Name *three* diseases against which babies are immunised and *one* disease
           against which teenagers are immunised.

       ii) Name *one* disease against which you cannot be immunised.

       iii) Why is it important that girls are immunised against German measles
            (rubella) in their early teens?

9 Read this passage and then answer the questions below:

   > Joseph Lister was a nineteenth-century surgeon who introduced antiseptic
   > methods into surgery. Before an operation he had all the instruments washed in
   > carbolic acid. During the operation a fine spray of carbolic acid was kept on the
   > area being treated. (All nursing staff were required to wash their hands with
   > carbolic soap before and after touching any patient.)

   a) i) What happened to many patients following operations in the nineteenth
           century?

       ii) What did Lister suspect to be the cause of this?

   b) i) What is an antiseptic?

       ii) What was the antiseptic which Lister used?

   c) Explain the reasons for each of the following:

       i) 'The instruments were washed in carbolic acid.'

       ii) 'During the operation, a fine spray of carbolic acid was kept on the area
           being treated.'

       iii) 'Staff were required to wash their hands with carbolic soap before and
            after touching any patient.'

   d) Modern surgery does not use the same methods as those of Lister. Instead the
       instruments and the apparatus are kept sterile.

       i) What does 'sterile' mean

       ii) Suggest two ways in which the instruments could be sterilised.

10 Read the two passages a) and b) and answer the questions on each passage.

a)   In 1928 Professor Alexander Fleming discovered that a mould found growing on a bacterial plate produced a substance that killed the bacteria on the plate. He went on to find out that this substance produced by the mould had the power of destroying all kinds of bacteria that cause human disease. He identified the mould as *Penicillium notatum*.

Fleming injected this bacteriocidal substance into mice and found that it did them no harm. However he also found that the substance lost its power to kill bacteria if kept for any length of time.

i)   Explain the following:

mould   bacterial plate   bacteriocidal

ii)   What name was given to the substance produced by the mould?

iii)   Try to find out more about how Alexander Fleming made his discovery.

b)   Surprisingly, there was very little interest in Fleming's discovery. It was not until 1938 that two scientists from Oxford called Florey and Chain repeated Fleming's experiments. They obtained the same results and also showed that the substance could kill harmful bacteria which had been injected into mice.

Most of their tests were completed by 1940, and because it was now wartime there was an urgent need for such a drug. Many scientists worked to find a way of making and preserving it in a new pure form. Eventually they succeeded and it began to be made commercially.

i)   Why is it surprising that there was no interest in Fleming's discovery for ten years?

ii)   How might Florey and Chain have shown that 'the substance could kill harmful bacteria which had been injected into mice'.

iii)   Why was there an urgent need in wartime for a drug with the power to kill bacteria?

iv)   What name is given to all substances that are produced by microbes and have the power to kill bacteria?

v)   Give another example of such a substance.

vi)   Name *two* diseases that can now be easily cured by these drugs but would probably have caused death 60 years ago.

11 Substance X is extracted from a living organism. The diagram opposite shows the effect it has on bacteria growing on agar jelly. Disc A has been soaked in a high concentration of X; disc B has been soaked in a low concentration of X; disc C was soaked in distilled water only. The three discs were placed on the surface of the agar jelly using sterile forceps. Bacteria had already been introduced into the agar jelly. The agar plate with the three discs in position was incubated for eighteen hours at 37 °C.

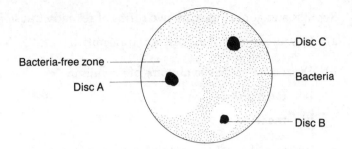

a) Why was disc C included in the experiment?

b) What effect does X appear to have on bacterial growth?

c) By what process would substance X get into the agar?

d) What is the general name given to a substance such as X?

e) Name one specific example of a substance that has properties similar to X's.

12 Study the diagram below of a particularly disgusting grocer's shop and its staff toilet.

If you were a Public Health Inspector, what changes would you insist on in order to make this shop more hygienic?

13 Syphilis and gonorrhoea are two forms of sexually transmitted diseases.

a) How are each of these diseases transmitted?

b) What are the early symptoms of syphilis in

  i)   the male?

  ii)   the female?

c) What are the early symptoms of gonorrhoea in

  i)   the male?

  ii)   the female?

d) What happens if gonorrhoea is not treated?

e) What type of disease organism causes

  i)   syphilis?

  ii)   gonorrhoea?

f) How can the spread of the two diseases be prevented?

g) The following graphs show changes in the incidence of syphilis and gonorrhoea in England and Wales.

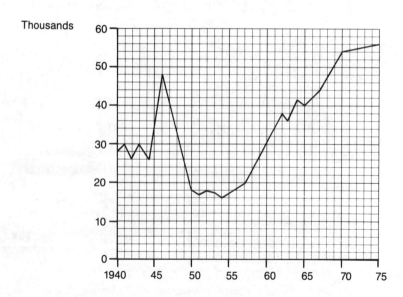

Incidence of gonorrhoea in England and Wales 1940–75

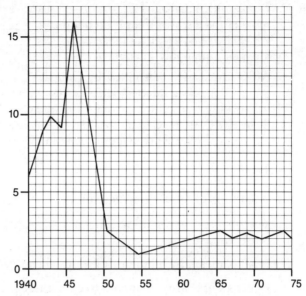

Incidence of infectious syphilis 1940–75

   i)   About how many cases of gonorrhoea and syphilis were recorded in 1950?

   ii)   Why did the incidence of the two diseases reach a peak just after the world war of 1939–45?

   iii) Why did the incidence of the diseases fall so quickly in the late 1940s and early 1950s?

   iv) Why has the incidence of syphilis remained steady since this time?

   v)   Suggest *two* reasons why gonorrhoea has become more common since the 1950s.

   vi) From the graphs predict the number of people in England and Wales who are likely to suffer from each of the diseases in 1990.

h)   Name one other disease which is sexually transmitted.

14 Copy and complete this passage about the Acquired Immune Deficiency Syndrome (AIDS). Fill in the gaps with words from the following list. (If necessary you may use a word more than once.)

         skin   placenta   sexual   lungs   immune
         Human Immunodeficiency Virus   blood   pneumonia
         lymphocytes   chicken pox   AIDS   milk   needles

a)   AIDS is caused by a virus called the _____. In humans this virus attacks and destroys _____. These cells help to protect us from diseases, such as _____ and _____.

People with a damaged _____ system are more likly to suffer from one or more of the diseases. People do not die of _____. They die from diseases which their bodies can no longer fight. The _____, _____ and brain are most commonly infected.

AIDS is usually transmitted by intimate _____ contact, or when the _____ of an infected person mixes with the _____ of someone else. It is readily transmitted among drug addicts who share _____ to inject themselves. An infected mother can pass AIDS onto her baby, either across the _____ during pregnancy or later in the _____ during breast feeding.

Now answer these questions.

b)   What type of cells in the body produce antibodies?

c)   Describe *two* ways in which antibodies help to destroy organisms that cause disease.

d)   What is meant by a high risk group when referring to AIDS?

e)   Which people are considered to be in these high risk groups and why?

f)   What precautions can be taken to restrict the spread of AIDS?

g)   Many scientists have predicted that a vaccine will not be available until at least the year 2000.

    i)   Why does it take so long to develop such a vaccine?

    ii)   What characteristic of the HIV means that it will be very difficult to produce a vaccine against AIDS?

5 Parasites and Humans

1   Explain the following terms:

      parasite   **host**   **vector**

2   Name a parasite of humans which is

  a)   a protoctistan

  b)   a flatworm

  c)   a roundworm

  d)   a fungus

  e)   an insect

3 a)   Head-lice and fleas are *ectoparasites*. What does this mean?

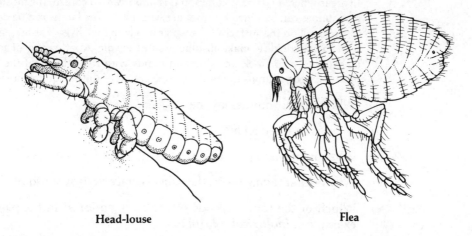

Head-louse   **Flea**

b)   Name one other ectoparasite.

c)   Look at the picture of the head-louse. It is well adapted for its life as a parasite. Its mouthparts are specialised to suck blood from the host for food and its body is flattened to help it move between the hairs. What other feature can you see that helps it to live among the hairs?

   i)   Where do head-lice lay their eggs? What are they called?

   ii)   Why are head-lice common parasites of young children?

   iii)   If you happen to catch head-lice, how can you get rid of them?

d)   Explain how a flea is adapted for its life as a parasite.

e)   What serious disease is transmitted from rats to man by the rat flea?

f)   What is an endoparasite? Name one.

4 a)   Why does malaria only occur in hot countries?

b)   Copy and complete this sentence:

   The malarial _____ is carried from person to person by the *Anopheles* _____ , which is the _____ of the disease.

c)   How would you protect yourself against malaria if you were visiting a country where the disease occurs?

d)   If someone came back into this country from abroad with malaria, would he or she need to be isolated? Explain your answer.

e) Read this paragraph and then answer the questions.

> In areas where malaria is common it is important to control the mosquito. Adult mosquitoes can be killed by spraying with DDT. The larvae can be destroyed by spraying oil on the surface of the water in which they live . The oil may be mixed with an insecticide to make absolutely sure they die. Another way of getting rid of mosquitoes is to stock up lakes and ponds with fish which eat the larvae and pupae. Or the swamps can be drained to get rid of the mosquito's breeding area.

   i)   Where do mosquitoes lay their eggs?

   ii)   What is an insecticide?

   iii) What are the dangers of using DDT to control mosquitoes?

   iv)   Why does spraying oil on the water surface destroy mosquito larvae?

   v)   Which of the four methods of control mentioned in the passage is an example of *biological control*?

   vi)   What are the advantages of using biological methods of control?

f) Other methods of combating malaria have been developed. These include i) drugs to kill the parasite in the blood and ii) vaccination to promote antibodies in the blood.

   In spite of a massive programme of malarial control, little progress has been made in eradicating the disease.

   Suggest why each of the methods discussed in this question may have failed.

5 a) Explain how each of the following helps the tapeworm to survive:

   i)   The head has hooks and suckers attached to it.

   ii)   Pork and beef are common foods of humans.

   iii) Tapeworms are hermaphrodite.

   iv)   Vast numbers of eggs are produced.

   v)   The body covering is resistant to digestion.

   vi)   Tapeworms can tolerate low oxygen levels.

b) The tapeworm does not possess a digestive system. Suggest a reason for this.

c) Draw a diagram to show the life cycle of the beef (or pork) tapeworm.

d) What precautions can be taken

   i)   by an individual

   ii)   by the community

   to prevent infection by tapeworms?

6 Insects, Useful and Harmful

1 Name *five* insects that are useful to humans, and explain how they are useful. Present the information in a table with these headings.

Name of insect	Use to humans

2 Explain how the following insects are harmful to humans:

> **locust**   **mosquito**   **flea**   **clothes-moth**   **house-fly**   **greenfly**
> **cabbage-white butterfly**   **furniture beetle**

Present the information in a table with these headings.

Name of insect	Why it is a pest

7 Social Insects

1 a) Why are some insects called 'social' insects?

   b) Name *four* social insects.

2 a) Name *one* social insect that is useful to humans. Explain why it is useful.

   b) Name *one* social insect that is harmful to humans. Explain why it is harmful.

3 a) Copy and complete this table about the honey-bee. The first row has been done for you.

Type (caste) of bee	Sex	What gametes does it produce, if any?	Main food	Function(s) within the colony
Queen	female	eggs	royal jelly	1. to lay all the eggs 2. to unite the colony 3. to start new colonies by swarming
Worker				
Drone				

b) Write a few sentences about each of the following:

   i)   hive

   ii)   combs

   iii)   honey

   iv)   royal jelly

   v)   queen substance

   vi)   swarm

   vii)   marriage flight

   viii)   waggle dance